super juice

michael van straten

super juice

juicing for health & healing

Bounty
BOOKS

Dedication

This book is dedicated with apologies to Sally Pearce, who put up with four months of a very strange existence. Like ships that pass in the night, we were seldom in the same place and awake at the same time. As always, Sally has been the epitome of patience and understanding, and the provider of late-night sandwiches. Our communication was largely messages scrawled on bottles of the latest juice creation. Without her taste buds, some of my stranger and less-palatable concoctions might well have found their way into this volume.

MvS

An Hachette UK Company
www.hachette.co.uk

First published in Great Britain in 1999 by Mitchell Beazley,
an imprint of the Octopus Publishing Group Ltd
Carmelite House, 50 Victoria Embankment, London EC4Y 0DZ
www.octopusbooks.co.uk

This edition published in 2017 by Bounty Books,
an imprint of Octopus Publishing Group Ltd

ISBN 978-0-7537-3102-4

A CIP catalogue record for this book is available from the British Library.

Printed and bound in China

10 9 8 7 6 5 4 3 2 1

Superjuice is meant to be used as a general recipe book. While the author believes the recipes it contains are beneficial to health, the book is in no way intended to replace medical advice. You are urged to consult a physician about specific medical complaints and the use of healing herbs and foods in the treatment thereof.

Although all reasonable care has been taken during the preparation of this edition, the publisher, editor and author cannot accept responsibility for any consequences arising from its use or from the information it contains.

Commissioning Editor: Margaret Little
Editor: Jamie Ambrose
Design and illustrations: Grace Helmer
Cover design: Megan van Staden
Photography: William Reavell
Home economist: Laura Fyfe
Senior Production Manager: Peter Hunt

contents

introduction

The first edition of this book was published in 1999, and how things have changed in the last 15 years! Sadly, many of these changes have been for the worse. Anyone who has the slightest interest in health can't fail to be aware of the epidemic of Type 2 diabetes – the condition caused by bad diet, lack of exercise and obesity – particularly in children. There has also been a decline in physical activity among all ages.

More than ever there is a need for simple, safe and inexpensive ways to safeguard our health and vitality. We all need to support our innate natural defences and counteract the adverse effects of the chemicals in the air we breathe and the water we drink. It has to be said that juicing isn't the panacea for all that ails us, but in my experience it's certainly a giant step on the road to good health for you and your family.

Juicing has a strong history. During the first half of the last century, fresh fruit and vegetable juices were the mainstay of spas in continental Europe and health farms in the UK and US. Juices were widely known as the building blocks of health and vitality. Maybe it's no surprise that the food industry saw a golden opportunity – the explosion of juice-based products in our supermarkets produced vast profits, but they're at your expense. Who pays for all the advertising for those drinks and smoothies, which are often only 10 per cent juice? You do.

Even when the manufacturers say that their juices or smoothies are 'fresh', they could be made from concentrates or have sat in a warehouse for days, losing vitamin C. Your own fresh juices – free from additives causing asthma, eczema and hyperactivity, especially in children – boost energy, vitality and immunity. Juicing also protects vital, life-enhancing nutrients, so you get maximum benefit from your fruit and vegetables. Peeled and cooked, these natural wonders lose much of their value, even more so when juice is pasteurized, concentrated and preserved.

I am appalled by the explosion of 'celebrity' juice-based diets. Followers of magic weight-loss plans put their health at risk and set themselves up for disappointment. A lengthy juice diet will not achieve long-term results, as you quickly regain the weight lost. Prolonged juice-only regimes can cause bad breath, tooth damage, hair loss and a lack of vital nutrients. The Superjuice Detox on page 154, however, will do no harm and lots of good.

As a naturopath, I've advised my patients to make their own juices for 50 years. But it wasn't until I visited Australia and spent an afternoon in a juicing bar, choosing from fantastic mixes of fruits and vegetables, that I knew this book was for fun as well as health. If you want to feel better, get well and look great, have better skin and lose some weight, this book is your health Bible. Have a drink on me. Cheers!

juicing: a practical guide

What to juice

Juicing is a simple, fun and fast way to add huge amounts of
nutrients and protective plant chemicals to your daily diet.
You can juice just about any fruit, vegetable or herb. To get the
maximum amount of vitamins, minerals, enzymes and amazing
plant chemicals into your body, buy organic produce whenever
possible, particularly when making juice for babies and small
children. The best juice comes from the freshest produce.

Wash ingredients thoroughly, scrubbing tough-skinned varieties
with a soft brush. As substantial amounts of minerals lie
just below the peel, all fruits and vegetables should be juiced
with their skins on, except where otherwise stated – bananas,
pineapples, mangoes, passion-fruit and pretty well all citrus
fruits need to have their skins removed. Non-organic produce
should be washed in a solution of one teaspoon of washing-up
liquid to a litre of warm water and then rinsed thoroughly – this
removes most external pesticides, fungicides and waxes. To
avoid unnecessary vitamin loss, don't chop produce before you
need it. When juicing small quantities of ingredients – six mint
leaves, a small piece of ginger and a few sage leaves, for instance
– wrap them in one of the other ingredients first. When making
smoothies, put ice in the liquidizer with a little water and switch
on for a few seconds before adding the other ingredients.

Once you get the hang of jucing, you'll want to experiment with your own concoctions – be as inventive as you like. I have only one rule for would-be Superjuicers: NEVER hide your machine in a cupboard. Once put away, it will stay there for years without seeing a single carrot or apple. Find a space on the worktop so that your juicer will always be ready for action.

Choosing the best machine

It is best to have a separate juicer and liquidizer – a juicer separates the pulp from the liquid it extracts from your fruit and vegetables, while a liquidizer blends all the ingredients together, making it perfect for smoothies. Citrus attachments are available for most juicers, or you can buy a separate citrus fruit juicer, which is often cheaper and easier. When making combinations, it is better to peel citrus fruits and put them through a juicer with the other ingredients.

Less expensive machines are excellent now (you can buy a juicer for under £100), but top-of-the-range models last longer and extract more juice. If you're a beginner and want to dip your toe in the water, start with an inexpensive machine and see how you get on. Look for a machine that is easy to use, feels robust and is simple to take apart and clean.

how to use this book

First and foremost, *Superjuice* is a recipe book: a collection
of different ways of combining ingredients. Some recipes
are obvious, some are unusual and others are rather strange,
but they're all here for a purpose. Don't dismiss a recipe
just because it seems 'alien' at first sight! You won't find
meaningless figures in *Superjuice*. Instead, simple descriptions
show the vitamins and minerals contained in each recipe, which
makes one 225 ml (8 fl oz) glass of juice:

Super-rich Contains more than 50 per cent of the daily requirement
Rich Contains 25–50 per cent of the daily requirement
Contains Contains 10–25 per cent of the daily requirement

Other than where specifically stated, all relative proportions
listed in recipes are approximate. In addition, quantities
of ingredients will vary according to their size, variety and
ripeness; some apples are bigger than others, after all! With
a bit of practise, you'll soon become an expert at judging how
many carrots or apples yield 225 ml (8 fl oz) of juice.

The book is divided into two sections. The first (and largest) is devoted to enhancing the life you already lead. It begins with recipes for juices that boost energy levels, followed by a cleansing section which shows how to detox your system quickly and successfully; this helps to eliminate the toxic by-products of the typical Western diet. Then come chapters on juices designed specifically to improve vitality, enhance your immune system – even boost your sex drive.

The second part of the book deals with the curative powers of juicing, beginning with The Natural Pharmacy (see page 142) and including a list of all the vitamins and minerals present in the raw ingredients used in the recipes. In the Drink Yourself Better tables (see page 150), you can choose a juice to treat specific illnesses. The second section concludes with a Superjuice Detox (see page 154) which shows how to rid your body of all the harmful elements derived from modern living.

power juices

In today's world, everyone needs energy and stamina: power to make it through the day, to cope with the uncertainties of job security, the rigours of bringing up a family and the monthly tyranny of rent or mortgage. Power juices provide the answer.

For energy and stamina, you need good calories, and you'll find them in abundance in Power Juices, together with the nutrients that are essential for their conversion into usable energy. It is said that 70 per cent of the UK's population wakes up tired every morning; that doesn't bode well for the rest of the day. Many people rely on the artificial stimulus provided by caffeine and sugar to give them a boost, munching chocolate bars on the way to work and drinking even more sweet tea or coffee when they arrive. Add mid-morning sticky buns, washed down by yet more caffeine, and it's no wonder that most experience a sinking feeling before they even get to lunchtime.

A Power Juice for breakfast will get you off to a flying start. Try Pumping Iron (see page 23), or Instant Energizer (see page 14). If you need mental energy for a meeting, interview or exam, boost your brain power with High Flyer (see page 15). For sport after work or Saturday on the golf course, kick off with Peak Performer (see page 17).

Note to the calorie conscious: while Power Juices provide both physical and mental energy, they are not remedies for an unbalanced diet or continual low-calorie weight-loss diets. Any slimming regime that depends on a 1,000-calorie-a-day input is doomed to disaster. Within a week or 10 days, your nutritional intake will have fallen so much that you would be at risk of deficiency, and the tiredness and irritability that result inevitably lead you to binge. You instantly gain more weight than you've lost, and end up feeling guilty into the bargain. A sensible eating plan that reduces fat and sugar consumption, supplemented with Power Juices, is the sensible way to achieve weight loss. For a little extra help in getting started on a sensible weight-loss programme, see the Superjuice Detox on page 154.

instant energizer

There is no better way to start your day than with instant calories and enough protection to fight off bugs for 24 hours. The Instant Energizer provides a glassful of brain power and heart-strengtheners, along with gentle stimulants to purge excess fluid which accumulates overnight. Puffy feet and fingers will be gone before you leave home. This is also an ideal juice for women who experience fluid retention before their periods.

carrots 4, unpeeled; unless organic, remove top and bottom

apple 1, unpeeled, uncored and quartered

kiwi fruit 1, peeled

parsley 1 handful, with stems

vital statistics

Super-rich in **vitamins A, C, E**. Rich in **B vitamins** and **potassium**. Potassium is vital for the normal balance of water in the body, and it's essential in the production of enzymes which stimulate energy production. It's also part of the mechanism that keeps the heart beating regularly. The carotenoids in carrots and parsley improve night vision, keep eyes healthy and are great for skin. Finally, the Instant Energizer is full of **antioxidants** which protect against heart disease and some cancers.

high flyer

If you've a busy day ahead and little chance of a good meal until the evening, set yourself up with this blood-building, vitamin-laden energy-booster. A massive health-protector and life-extender, the High Flyer should be on everyone's menu at least twice a week. This brain-booster will keep your mental faculties in top gear. As a bonus, it slows skin ageing. It also prevents sun damage, so should be taken regularly before holidays.

spinach 6 leaves

carrots 3, unpeeled; unless organic, remove top and bottom

apple 1, unpeeled, uncored and quartered

beetroot 1 medium, unpeeled, with leaves

vital statistics

Super-rich in **carotenes** and **potassium**. Rich in **vitamin C**. Contains **B vitamins**. A Superjuice for mental energy. The red colour in beetroot is similar to that of haemoglobin in blood and is a traditional treatment for anaemia, leukaemia and cancer in Eastern Europe. By increasing the oxygen-carrying power of blood, it also increases **brain power**, **concentration** and **memory**.

the red-eye special

Taken the overnight plane? Been burning the midnight oil?
Had a night on the tiles? Whatever the reason, the next day
can be hell – but it needn't be. While the Red-eye Special won't
work miracles, it comes pretty close. The ingredients in this
Superjuice were popular with ancient Greeks and Romans,
who knew that the natural oils in parsley and mint soothe the
stomach and calm jangley nerves. With clear eyes, no headache
and no puffiness or gritty skin, you'll get through the day in
better shape than you ever imagined possible.

mint 6 leaves, with stems

spinach 6 leaves

melon 1 medium, yellow-fleshed, peeled and deseeded

parsley 1 handful, with stems

vital statistics
Super-rich in **potassium** and **vitamin A**.
The Red-eye Special is a detoxifying juice, thanks to the
parsley it contains. Both parsley and mint have a healing
effect on the digestive system and are calming to the central
nervous system. Melon juice also overflows with healing
beta-carotenes and is exceptionally curative and
cooling. Two or three glasses of this juice throughout the
day will see you through until bedtime, then sleep will add
the finishing touches.

peak performer

Never underestimate the power of pears! Few people realize the nutritional value that may be found in a ripe pear of any variety – and the juice adds a unique flavour to this Superjuice. Even just sniffing its wonderful aroma helps set the stage for a real feel-good day. If you're feeling a bit sluggish, then the soluble fibre found in the pears and apples – together with the rich supply of natural sugars in grapes and pineapple – are just the thing to aid digestion and provide instant energy.

grapes 12, black or white

pears 4, unpeeled

apples 2, unpeeled, uncored and quartered

pineapple 2 slices, peeled

vital statistics
Rich in **potassium**, **pectin** (soluble fibre) and **natural healing enzymes**. Contains **vitamin C**, **calcium** and traces of **B vitamins**. In addition to its wealth of vitamins and nutrients, the Peak Performer has other health benefits to offer. The tannins, powerful flavones and other aromatic compounds harboured in grapes combine to become **energizing** and cancer-fighting – all this in a Superjuice that tastes as great as it smells!

primary pepper punch

A juice to take on a regular basis. Don't be put off if you find green peppers acidic and indigestible: ripe red and yellow peppers are deliciously sweet and succulent. What's more, they combine beautifully with the other vegetables to make this a cocktail with a difference. You'll obtain ultimate antioxidant power from the massive dose of beta-carotenes and other carotenoids that colour these vibrant vegetables.

carrots 2, unpeeled; unless organic, remove top and bottom

beetroot 1 small, unpeeled, with leaves

celery 1 stick, with leaves

yellow pepper ½, deseeded

red pepper ½, deseeded

vital statistics
Super-rich in **beta-carotene**, **vitamins A** and **C**, **folic acid** and **potassium**. The iron-rich beet tops help prevent anaemia, so this is a primary Power Juice for women. It's also a real pollution-fighter that declares war on the damaging free radicals present in our environment, so it's especially good for city-dwellers. Of course, there are internal pollutants, too, and if you must smoke, this colourful cocktail will at least give you some increased protection against lung cancer.

boxer's beverage

One glass of this Superjuice packs the punch of Muhammad Ali. Overflowing with instantly available essential nutrients, Boxer's Beverage provides power, energy and stamina. The minerals, vitamins and easily utilized calories make this the perfect partner for a high-carbohydrate snack taken shortly before physical exercise. This juice is also a great reviver after strenuous exertion.

carrots 4, unpeeled; unless organic, remove top and bottom

kiwi fruit 1, unpeeled

parsley 1 handful, with stems

spinach 1 handful of leaves

vital statistics
Super-rich in **vitamins A, C, E, B$_6$, folic acid** and **potassium**. Rich in other **B vitamins** and **iron**. Contains calcium. Truly a first-class Superjuice for boxers and non-boxers alike! One glass provides more than your daily requirement of all the vitamins and minerals listed above. Great for building up body power in advance of taxing times (physical or mental) and ideal for replacing it during calmer phases.

horse power

It may sound simple, but this classic apple-and-carrot mixture, spiked with fresh horseradish, is fuel for any bucking bronco. You will derive instant energy derived from the natural sugars in the carrots and apples, but the horseradish adds a whole new dimension. You'll get very little juice and lots of pulp from 85 g (3 oz) of horseradish, but what you do get is instant stimulation of the circulation. With the blood coursing through the veins, you'll be ready for anything.

carrots 4, unpeeled; unless organic, remove top and bottom

apples 2, unpeeled, uncored and quartered

horseradish 85 g (3 oz) fresh

vital statistics

Super-rich in **vitamins A, C, E, potassium** and **vitamin B$_6$**. Contains some **calcium** and traces of other **B vitamins**. Even this most simple of Superjuices is bursting with good stuff. With just under 300 calories a glass, it's a good quick-energy source. In addition, horseradish contains the natural substance **sinigrin**, a powerful antibiotic that protects against infection.

melon and mango tango

This cool, refreshing drink will kick-start your metabolism and help you shrug off that early morning sluggishness. One glass and you'll be running at full power throughout the day.

mango 1, peeled and stoned

melon ½, yellow-fleshed

(cantaloupe, ogen or muskmelon),

peeled and deseeded

vital statistics

Super-rich in **vitamins A** and **C**. This juice provides more than your daily needs of both vitamins listed above. Used for centuries as a diuretic in India, melon helps to redude morning puffiness. As a bonus, melon also contains **adenosine**, a substance that makes blood less sticky, thus reducing the risk of blood clots and heart attack. A super-rich source of **instant energy** and nutrients, the mango has been cultivated and eaten for more than 4,000 years. The combined vitamin A content of melon and mango juice is a boost to the immune system and helps protect the body from cancer.

spinach spectacular

This is the perfect midday power booster. Taken with a light lunch, it will see you through a mentally or physically arduous afternoon and still leave you with reserves for an evening out.

apple 1, unpeeled, uncored and quartered

celery 1 stick, with leaves

spinach 85 g (3 oz) fresh young leaves

watercress 1 handful

vital statistics

Super-rich in vitamins **A**, **C** and **folic acid**. Rich in **riboflavin (B$_2$)**. While a certain sailor-man ate it for iron, spinach is hard to make the most of due to the high levels of oxalic acid in its leaves which stop absorption of iron. Placed in this Superjuice, however, the huge amounts of other vitamins and nutrients it contains would have given Popeye **superpowers** even he never dreamt of!

pumping iron

Here's a power-pumping iron tonic in a glass for those dull, grey days when you just can't seem to charge up the batteries. It's all too easy to dismiss the cucumber as nothing more than water. While its nutritional content is very low, it is nonetheless regarded as an important healing vegetable in natural medicine – which explains why it appears in lots more recipes. Here, the cucumber's cool, refreshing flavour contrasts superbly with the astringency of beetroot, spinach and watercress.

apples 2, unpeeled, uncored and quartered
beetroot 1 small, unpeeled, with leaves
cucumber 1 medium
spinach 1 handful of leaves
watercress 1 handful

vital statistics
Super-rich in **iron**, **vitamin C** and **folic acid**.
Rich in **beta-carotene** and other carotenoids. The vitamin C in this Superjuice makes the iron it contains all the more easily absorbed by the body, while its beta-carotene and other **carotenoids** protect against cancers. All this, plus its instant supply of natural sugars, makes Pumping Iron the perfect juice for serious exercisers, vegetarians and women planning pregnancy.

green apple power punch

A zappy cleanser to start your day, the Green Apple Power Punch is ideal for stimulating the digestive system and replacing lost minerals following physical activity – on or off the sports field. Take this on an empty stomach and don't eat or drink anything else for half an hour to let its natural fruit sugars do their work.

sorrel 6 leaves

apples 2 large Granny Smith, unpeeled, uncored and quartered

lime 1, peeled (unless key lime)

mint 1 sprig, with stems

parsley 1 handful, with stems

vital statistics

Super-rich in **vitamins A, C, E, B$_6$** and **folic acid**. Rich in **magnesium** and **potassium**. Contains some calcium and iron. Soluble fibre in apples and natural oils in mint have a wonderful effect on the entire digestive system, as they are soothing and cause a gentle laxative effect. Sorrel has been used by Native Americans for centuries as an anti-cancer remedy; the lime's natural pigment, known as limonene, protects against cancer, too. Try this one for some real **health power** in a glass.

mediterranean muscle

Throughout the southern Mediterranean, the combination of tomatoes and basil is inseparable, not only for taste but also for the wonderful mixture of aromas. This Superjuice is another variation on the theme designed for mind and body: it's rich in minerals to give renewed vigour to tired muscles, and contains essential oils from the basil that act specifically on tired minds. Serve with a dash of Worcestershire sauce and some black pepper as a finishing touch.

plum tomatoes 4 large, ripe

carrot 1, unpeeled; unless organic, remove top and bottom

celery 1 stick, with leaves

basil 1 handful

lemon juice of ½, squeezed into finished juice

vital statistics
Super-rich in **vitamins A**, **C**, **E**, **folic acid** and **potassium**. Rich in **iron** and **magnesium**. Low in calories, Mediterranean Muscle is a perfect start to the day for anyone watching their weight. It also gets a five-star rating for peak power of mind and body, and is delicious, calming and mildly diuretic to boot. As a final bonus, this Superjuice contains lycopene, one of the most powerful natural antioxidants which protects specifically against heart disease.

cleansing juices

Most of us are familiar with the saying, 'cleanliness is next to godliness'. To the early 20th-century traditional health practitioner, this adage also applied to internal hygiene. Almost a century before 'detox' regimes came into fashion, detoxification was already a key practice of natural medicine.

Modern pollution, toxic waste and chemically treated and processed food make a cleansing regime more vital than ever for good health. By drinking Cleansing Juices, practising simple fasting and avoiding foods that overload the system, you can achieve dramatic results in your overall wellbeing. Clear eyes and skin, improved digestion, loss of surplus fluid, even a clearer mind... these are just some of the most quickly perceived benefits of inner cleansing. All the juices in this section are designed to improve the efficiency of the body's natural 'housekeeping system'. The recipes use the gentle power of natural foods to stimulate specific organs and functions. The juice of citrus fruits stimulates saliva glands, aiding the digestive process right from its beginnings in the mouth. Herbs and spices increase production of the stomach's digestive juices to ensure the proper breakdown of food and absorption of vitamins, minerals and micro-nutrients. Some Cleansing Juices also gently stimulate natural contractions of the bowel, thus helping to efficiently eliminate waste. Jerusalem artichokes, radishes and dandelions all increase the flow of bile, activate the liver and improve the digestion of fats. In some recipes, celery, parsley, dandelion leaves, lettuce and chicory are used to stimulate the kidneys and deal with fluid retention. Carrots cleanse the skin from the inside outwards. Once you've experienced the feeling of lightness, alertness and inner cleanliness these juices produce, you'll be a firm detox fan. Soon, you'll feel confident enough to tackle the complete Superjuice Detox on page 154.

Whether it's a specific problem such as spots or fluid retention, or just a general bloating, sluggishness or malaise, Cleansing Juices make ideal rescue remedies.

minty morning

A variation on what has to be the most popular breakfast juice of all. By combining the health-giving properties of oranges with the natural oils present in mint (the best digestive of all the members of the herb family), this juice makes a powerful digestive aid and cleanser that gets to work right from the start. If you're making this juice in a citrus-fruit juicer (see page 9), just halve the oranges, juice them, then chop the mint finely and stir it into the juice. If using a regular juicer, peel the oranges, remove most of the pith and feed small bunches of mint leaves into the machine between each two or three pieces of orange.

oranges 4 large, peeled, but leaving pith on

mint 1 generous sprig, with stems

vital statistics
Super-rich in **vitamin C**. Contains **potassium**, **calcium**, **folic acid** and **bioflavonoids**. Oranges boost overall resistance and are good for the heart and circulatory system. In natural medicine, they are also considered beneficial to the intestines, as they make it difficult for unwanted bacteria to survive. They also help with unpleasant problems such as constipation and wind. Like most citrus fruits, oranges stimulate the flow of saliva.

waterfall

Another powerful diuretic juice. Waterfall's combination of celery and parsley will help ease even the most stubborn fluid retention. Although English curly parsley is fine for this recipe, the European flat-leafed variety has a richer, fuller and slightly smoother flavour and is, if anything, an even better diuretic.

carrots 3, unpeeled; unless organic, remove top and bottom

apples 2, unpeeled, uncored and quartered

celery 2 sticks, with leaves

parsley 1 handful, with stems

vital statistics
Super-rich in **vitamins A, C, E** and **folic acid**. Rich in **potassium** and **magnesium**. Waterfall is a powerful medicine. As well as its strong diuretic effect, it's also a Superjuice that will benefit the skin and is ideal for anyone with high blood pressure or heart disease, since it is very low in sodium. It also makes a safe and excellent Cleansing Juice for use during pregnancy.

dandelion delight

When Grandma said picking the dandelions would make
you wet the bed, she wasn't exactly kidding. Dandelion leaves
are a powerful diuretic, and they are hugely popular as a salad
vegetable in France, where they are sold as *pis en lit salade*.
When combined with the natural fibre in the apple juice and
the skin-cleansing properties of carrots, this juice makes a
perfect cleanser.

dandelion leaves 6, well washed (or a handful of parsley if unavailable)

carrots 3, unpeeled, unless organic, remove top and bottom

apples 2, unpeeled, uncored and quartered

vital statistics
Super-rich in **vitamin A**. Rich in **vitamin C**.
Contains **iron**. Definitely not to be taken just before
leaving home! The effects of Dandelion Delight
may be apparent within half an hour and last for two,
which makes this is a good Cleansing Juice for women
around menstruation, as it helps eliminate general
puffiness and soothe painful, swollen breasts.

cleansing juices

women's wonder

When 'that time of the month' rolls around, it's time to down a glassful of this Superjuice. Women's Wonder is a powerful cleanser and, thanks to the fennel, contains phytoestrogens (plant hormones) which help regulate periods and bring some relief from PMS and menopausal symptoms. While this juice has been designed with women in mind, it's fine for men, too!

apples 2, unpeeled, uncored and quartered

carrots 2, unpeeled; unless organic, remove top and bottom

chicory 1 head

fennel ½ bulb

vital statistics

Super-rich in **vitamins A** and **C**. Rich in **folic acid** and **potassium**. Contains a good amount of **iron**. The cleansing power of Women's Wonder is due to the influence fennel and chicory exert on liver and kidney functions – perfect for easing the bloating that often accompanies periods. For women going through the menopause, its **phytoestrogens** act as a natural 'hormone replacement therapy' to help prevent bone loss and subsequent osteoporosis.

pepper purifier

In need of a powerful Superjuice to purify the system?
Then look no further than the Pepper Purifier – a particularly
important juice to be used after periods of illness that
necessitate medication. Taken on alternate days for a week,
it will help the body dispose of any drug residues.

carrots 3, unpeeled; unless organic, remove top and bottom

beetroot 1 small, unpeeled, with leaves

red pepper ½, deseeded

parsley 1 handful, with stems

spinach 1 handful of leaves

vital statistics
Super-rich in **vitamins A**, **C** and **E**. Rich in **folic acid**
and **potassium**. Contains useful amounts of some
B vitamins. The diuretic powers of parsley stimulate
the kidneys, while the fibre from the carrots and red pepper
stimulate the normal contractions of the large bowel,
hastening elimination. The combined blood-purifying
benefits of beetroot and spinach add the final touch to this
superb Cleansing Juice, which also replenishes the body's
stores of essential nutrients.

watermelon man

Naturopaths regard melon as a cooling cleanser, and in Indian Ayurvedic medicine it's used as an effective diuretic. It is also cooling to the body and soothing to the digestion. The addition of watercress, broccoli and the tart cooking apple make this 'green juice' a perfect cleanser for men, because it has a testosterone-enhancing effect. It's gently laxative and a powerful immune booster.

cooking apple 1, unpeeled, uncored and quartered
green melon ½, peeled and deseeded
broccoli florets 85 g (3 oz), without thick stems
watercress 1 handful

vital statistics
Rich in **vitamins A**, **C** and **E**. Contains **folic acid**, **magnesium** and **potassium**. This juice is particularly suitable for physically active men who enjoy regular sport (of course, women can take it, too). The mineral content will also replace losses experienced through sweating. As a regular Cleansing Juice taken once or twice weekly, the watercress and broccoli ensure a substantial intake of cancer-fighting nutrients.

rainbow cocktail

This mixture of orange, pink, green and yellow-skinned citrus fruits is both a liver and intestinal cleanser. Its clean, tangy taste also makes it a favourite anytime drink. Use the Rainbow Cocktail as an excellent start to a detox cleansing day. And if you are unfortunate enough to wake up with a hangover, then this cocktail works better than the hair of any dog!

oranges 2, peeled, but leaving pith on

lemon 1, with peel if thin-skinned

lime 1, peeled (unless key lime)

***pink grapefruit** 1, peeled, but leaving pith on

*If taking prescribed medicines, consult your doctor before drinking large amounts of grapefruit juice.

vital statistics
Super-rich in **vitamin C**. Rich in **vitamin A**. Contains a useful amount of **potassium** and **calcium**. The acidity of all these citrus fruit juices helps remove some of the unwanted bacteria from the digestive tract and encourages the growth of beneficial probiotic bacteria. Besides tasting terrific, the Rainbow Cocktail is a real digestive aid, which should be drunk for two or three days after a course of antibiotics to get your system back in good running order as soon as possible.

lemon express

Grapes are one of Nature's great cleansers. Because of their high natural sugar content, they should always feature in any detox regime. If you're cleansing your digestive system and reducing food consumption, the extra sugar will keep your energy levels up. The combination of grapes, soluble fibre in the apples and the gentle diuretic effect of the lemon makes this juice a particularly effective cleanser.

apples 3, unpeeled, uncored and quartered
lemon 1, with peel if thin-skinned
white grapes 115 g (4 oz)

vital statistics
Rich in **vitamin C**, **soluble fibre** and **natural sugars**. Contains **antioxidant bioflavonoids** and **potassium**. The pith of lemons is rich in a natural substance called **limonene**, now believed to have anti-cancer properties. For this reason, when making the Lemon Express, it's best to peel the lemon first, leaving on the white pith and then put it through your juicer, rather than using a citrus fruit juicer which leaves all the helpful pith behind.

prune–light express

Prunes have something of a bad press, but they are a 'natural'
natural ingredient to include in any cleansing regime – and they
taste terrific. This Superjuice boasts a slightly sweet-and-sour
edge and gives off that wonderful aroma of pears. The sharpness
of the apple will counteract the sweetness of the prunes.

pears 2, unpeeled
cooking apple 1 medium, unpeeled, uncored and quartered

Juice the above.

prunes 4, stoned, soaked overnight in water
water 125 ml (4 fl oz)

*Combine the above ingredients in a blender, then stir
into the finished juice.*

vital statistics
Rich in **vitamin C**. Contains a large amount
of soluble fibre in the form of **pectin** from the apple
and pears. The gentle bulking activity of the fibre,
combined with the laxative properties of prunes,
makes Prune-light Express a good all-round cleanser.
Its stimulating effect on the digestive system makes
it a gentle laxative, and the vitamin C it contains is
always good for the **immune system**.

ginger spice

Ginger Spice is a gentle cleanser which benefits from the powerful volatile oils zingiberene and gingerol present in the ginger, as well as the cleansing and digestive benefits of carrot, apple and orange. This Cleansing Juice has powerful antiseptic and anti-inflammatory benefits and is perfect to use at the onset of a cold or fever, or immediately after a bout of food poisoning.

carrots 2, unpeeled; unless organic, remove top and bottom

apple 1, unpeeled, uncored and quartered

orange 1, peeled, buy leaving pith on

ginger 25 g (1 oz), fresh root, peeled and sliced

vital statistics
Rich in **vitamins A**, **C** and **fibre**. Ginger is one of the most versatile and valuable of spices. The ancient Greeks used it for digestive problems and as an antidote to poisoning, while medieval herbalists valued its warming properties highly. In the many ginger recipes you'll find in this book, it also provides an invigorating lift – particularly in the Aphrodisiac Juices chapter!

radish revolution

The radish is a much-overlooked and highly valuable vegetable – so valuable, in fact, that the ancient pharaohs used radishes (along with garlic and onions) to pay the workers who built the pyramids in Egypt! A member of the cabbage family, radish also contains anti-cancer nutrients. Combined with the diuretic power of dandelion (or parsley) and the cleansing benefits of carrots, this sharp, peppery juice will revolutionize your cleansing programme.

carrots 6, unpeeled; unless organic, remove top and bottom

dandelion leaves 6, well washed (or a handful of parsley if unavailable)

radishes 4 medium, with leaves

vital statistics
Rich in **vitamin A**, **potassium** and **sulphur**. Contains some **vitamin C** and **selenium**. As part of this Cleansing Juice, radishes stimulate the gall bladder to increase the release of bile, and stimulate the liver. These properties combine to make Radish Revolution a real fat-buster – a Superjuice not to be missed from any detox programme.

jerusalem juice

If you've embarked on a cleansing regime that involves a day
or so of restricted food intake and Cleansing Juices, then this is
the Superjuice with which to start off your morning. Besides its
general cleansing properties, it'll keep your blood sugar on an
even keel, and the coriander helps suppress the rather flatulent
effects produced by the artichokes.

jerusalem artichokes 3, unpeeled, well scrubbed

carrots 2, unpeeled; unless organic, remove top and bottom

pear 1, unpeeled

coriander 1 handful

vital statistics
Rich in **vitamin A**. The combined effects of the **pectin**
from the pear, the **inulin** from the artichokes and the
cleansing aromatic oils from the coriander make this a real
powerhouse of a Cleansing Juice. Jerusalem artichokes are
the richest source of inulin: a type of sugar. While inulin is
not converted into energy, it is a great **stimulant** of the
immune system – a valuable asset while detoxing.

the florentine

Although Florence fennel (to give it its full name) has been grown for more than 2,000 years, it is more commonly used in England for its pale green fronds which go so well with fish. Yet with its unique taste and aroma of aniseed, the fennel bulb is also a gentle diuretic and digestive aid. Combined here with the sweeter carrot and fruit flavours, it makes a delicious and therapeutic mixture.

apples 2, unpeeled, uncored and quartered
pears 2, unpeeled
carrot 1, unpeeled; unless organic, remove top and bottom
fennel 1 medium bulb

vital statistics
Rich in **vitamins A** and **C**, **potassium**, and **pectin**. It is the volatile oils of **anisic acid** **fenchone** and **anethole** that give fennel its unique flavour as well as its diuretic, cleansing and digestive properties. Although fennel itself isn't bursting with nutrients, it more than makes up for this deficiency with its role as a potent purifier.

quartet in 'c'

The calorie conscious know that lettuce is 95 per cent water and has hardly any calories – yet its nutritional value is enough to surprise anyone. It harbours some vitamin C, beta-carotene, calcium, potassium, a little iodine, a little iron and substantial amounts of folic acid. Since it is also cleansing, cooling and mildly diuretic, lettuce makes this a special Cleansing Juice that is an ideal tonic for the digestive system, eyes and skin.

carrots 3, unpeeled; unless organic, remove top and bottom

cos lettuce 1, smallish

coriander 1 small bunch

chives 1 small bunch

vital statistics

Super-rich in **vitamin A** and **carotenoids**. Rich in **potassium** and **folic acid**. Contains useful amounts of **vitamin C**, **B vitamins**, **iron** and **iodine**. The antiseptic and antifungal sulphur compounds in the chives, the diuretic and calming oils in lettuce and the unique digestion-promoting constituents of coriander make Quartet in 'C' a highly potent mixture – the perfect note on which to end this Cleansing Juices chapter!

vitality juices

Almost two centuries ago, the doctrine of vitalism held that the origin and phenomena of life are the result of a vital principle – not just of purely chemical or physical forces. Vitality is that force: the captive dynamic power present in seeds, nuts, berries, fruits and vegetables.

Because they harness the forces of sunlight, earth and water, these growing things contain everything we need to live life to the full. To be healthy, active and mentally alert; to produce fine, strong children; to avoid the diseases of the modern world and unnecessary ill health in old age... all this and more is within everyone's grasp.

Designed as it is, the human body should survive in an active, healthy state for as much as 120 years. So why doesn't it? Part of the answer lies in the modern, hectic world we live in. Increased stress levels, sedentary jobs and greater pollution are all factors, but – more importantly – so is our diet. By moving away from natural foods with their inherent vitality, we have sold ourselves short. We may well be living longer than our ancestors, but we're having to deal with such diseases as cancer and chronic fatigue syndrome, CJD and Alzheimer's disease, arthritis and Parkinson's disease. I can't guarantee that you will avoid all these, but if you want to give the scales a massive tilt in your favour, then look no further than Vitality Juices.

These juices contain powerful antioxidant nutrients that neutralize dangerous free radicals. Some are laden with carotenoids that protect the eyes. Some are simply bursting with vitamin E, which promotes fertility. Others are rich in substances that protect against a wide variety of cancers. Does juicing really promote vitality? Well, a sprightly patient told me on his 90th birthday that he still had two ambitions in life. One was to get a centenary telegram from the Queen; the other was to be shot by a jealous husband. He has been Vitality Juicing for 50 years – so I'm not sure he was joking!

apple and watercress energizer

This is the ultimate vitality Superjuice, ideal as a regular booster once or twice a week, and essential at times of greater stress, increased workload or any time when your body and mind need to be bursting with vitality and creative energy. It also promotes greater concentration and is an aid to mental agility and physical activity – which is precisely why it's called the 'Energizer'.

apples 2, unpeeled, uncored and quartered

carrots 2 large, unpeeled; unless organic, remove top and bottom

tomatoes 2 medium, ripe

kiwi fruit 1, unpeeled

watercress 1 handful

spinach 1 handful of leaves

vital statistics
Super-rich in **vitamin C**. Rich in **vitamin A**, **beta-carotene**, **potassium**, **magnesium** and **zinc**. Contains **iron**, **calcium** and **lycopene**. Because of its high **vitamin C** content – more, in fact, than your minimum daily requirement – this juice will help ward off many a common cold or bout of the 'flu. Its lycopene guards against heart disease and cancer – not bad for something that is also a terrific booster juice!

apple tart

Here's an eye-opening Vitality Juice to start your day.
The sweetness of the apples and the acidity of the lemon
juice cleanse the palate, while the volatile esters provide
a head-clearing aroma that will get anyone off to a good start.
Experiment with different varieties and mixtures of apples.
The most aromatic will produce the greatest benefits.

apples 4, unpeeled, uncored and quartered
lemon 1, with peel if thin-skinned

vital statistics
Super-rich in **vitamin C**. Contains **bioflavonoids**
and **limonene**. 'An apple a day keeps the doctor away,'
says the proverb – and it's almost true. The special soluble
fibre in apples helps the body eliminate cholesterol, and
eating two a day is enough to make a measurable difference
in a short space of time. Even smelling the aroma of fresh
apples is enough to lower your blood pressure, and it can
sometimes prevent the onset of a migraine attack.

power pack

Pears, apples, celery, kiwi fruit: you'll search hard to find a juice that packs a more powerful punch in the vitality stakes than Power Pack. Never ignore the nutritional value of pears: they're much more than just a sweet fruit. Like apples, they're rich in pectin, easily digested and help the body eliminate cholesterol – all of which make this a highly valuable Vitality Juice.

apples 2, unpeeled, uncored and quartered

kiwi fruit 2, unpeeled

pears 2, unpeeled

celery 1 stick, with leaves

vital statistics

Super-rich in **vitamin C**, **beta-carotene** and other **carotenoids**. Rich in **vitamins A** and **E**. Contains **folic acid**, **potassium** and immune-boosting **phytochemicals**. The combined benefits of Power Pack make it a real stress-buster. The acids in apples break down fatty foods, while the huge amounts of carotenoids in kiwi fruit are protective and energy enhancing. Celery adds a calming effect, helping to eliminate stress and keeping blood pressure low; no wonder Hippocrates used it around 2,000 years ago for this very reason!

tropical revitalizer

It may be summertime, but in the city, the living ain't easy. With massive amounts of pollution-borne free radicals, bacteria and viruses pumping through air-conditioning systems, the office is a particularly dangerous place. But fear not! This Superjuice will boost your natural resistance and revitalize your energy levels. What's more, it tastes great: the sharp cooking apple contrasts with the sweetness of pineapple and mango, all of which blend beautifully with the berry flavours.

cooking apple 1 Bramley, unpeeled, uncored and quartered

mango 1, peele and stoned

pineapple ½, unpeeled

blueberries 115 g (4 oz)

strawberries 115 g (4 oz)

vital statistics
Super-rich in **vitamins A** and **C**, and **carotenoids**. The Tropical Revitalizer provides specific anti-cancer, antiviral and anti-bacterial substances which have a direct effect on the immune system. The healing enzymes in pineapple also make this a valuable Superjuice to take after physical activity, injury or surgery. And what better way to recharge the batteries on a hot summer's evening than with a glassful of something this fabulous?

blue passion

Here's a juice that is guaranteed to chase away the blues, put a glow on the skin and keep you super active. It looks good, tastes good and does you good because it overflows with masses of nutrients. Blue Passion is a real tonic: just one glass will give you instant energy and high levels of immunity. What better way to start the day?

passion fruit 3, seeds scooped out into juicer
cantaloupe melon 1 medium, peeled and deseeded
mango 1, peeled and stoned
blueberries 115 g (4 oz)

vital statistics
Super-rich in **vitamin A** and **C**. Rich in **carotenoids**. Contains **B vitamins** and **vitamin E**, **potassium** and some **calcium**. The abundant carotenoids are Blue Passion's most important asset: they're hugely protective against degenerative diseases and cancers, and also good for your eyes. This magical mixture is better than turning water into wine or lead into gold. It's a pity the alchemists never stumbled on this formula...

wrinkle zapper

Yes, I know. It's a pain taking the stones out of all those cherries, but it's well worth it: you end up with the most delicious juice you've ever tasted. Do make sure you choose dessert cherries rather than the cooking variety, however, which are very sour. Buy the darkest-coloured ones you can find, as they're the richest in the highly protective natural substances that make this such a valuable Vitality Juice.

apples 2, unpeeled, uncored and quartered
cherries 350 g (12 oz), stoned

vital statistics
Super-rich in **vitamin C**. Rich in **carotenoids**.
Contains **folic acid** and **potassium**. The real bonus
of this juice is its huge concentration of substances called
anthocyanidins and **proanthocyanidins** which
have powerful protective and regenerative properties
directly linked to collagen. You won't need those injections
if you consume regular amounts of the Wrinkle Zapper
– a much safer and cheaper alternative!

in the pink

The colloquial saying 'in the pink' means to be in very good health – and that's what this juice will help you to be. In the West, plums are not usually thought of as being particularly healthgiving, but Oriental medicine knows better. This simple, quick and delicious juice is an instant shot in the arm that's rich in blood-building vitality boosters.

red plums 6, stoned
red apples 2, unpeeled, uncored and quartered
***pink grapefruit** 2, peeled but leaving pith on

*If taking prescribed medicines, consult your doctor before drinking large amounts of grapefruit juice.

vital statistics
Super-rich in **vitamin C** and **bioflavonoids**.
Rich in **potassium** and **carotenes**. Thanks to the plums, In the Pink is also a valuable source of iron which can be easily absorbed due to its high **vitamin C** content. Make sure you peel the grapefruit carefully before juicing, however, leaving on as much pith as possible to preserve its vitality-enhancing **bioflavonoids** and **pectin**.

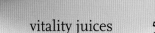

athlete's pitstop

This Vitality Juice is really the 'Wrinkle Zapper Mark II', but our American cousins will grasp the significance of this juice's name, since they call cherry stones 'pits'. Like the Wrinkle Zapper, Athlete's Pitstop is full of collagen-protecting substances that make this a boon for the regular athlete or exerciser, since collagen forms the building blocks of the cartilage, ligaments and tendons that are so prone to damage during sports.

apple 1, unpeeled, uncored and quartered
pear 1, unpeeled
cherries 350 g (12 oz), stoned

vital statistics
Super-rich in **vitamin C**. Rich in **carotenoids**. Contains **folic acid** and **potassium**. The slightly higher sugar content of the pear adds a little extra energy to this juice, so it's a useful vitality drink before or after exercise. Though the dark-green, thicker-skinned pears contain more fibre and pectin, the golden-yellow Williams version is sweeter, with more sugar. Either way, the **phytochemicals** this juice contains also protect all the collagen structures against damage and inflammation.

strawberry fayre

This juice is best made when strawberries are in season, since that's when they have their highest nutrient content. Pick your own strawberries or buy locally grown varieties whenever possible, as these delicate fruits don't travel well. Often thought of as too acidic and bad for arthritics, the truth is the exact opposite. Combined with the pear, peach and lemon, this is a 100-octane Vitality Juice.

peach 1, stoned

pear 1, unpeeled

lemon ½, with peel if thin-skinned

strawberries 450 g (1 lb)

vital statistics
Super-rich in **vitamin C**. Rich in **vitamins A** and **E**. Contains **potassium**. Due to the high contents of **natural salicylates** (aspirin-like substances) and **ellagic acid** contained in strawberries, this Vitality Juice is a natural, safe painkiller – especially good for all forms of arthritis. It is also a powerful anti-cancer mixture.

scarborough fair

Just like the traditional folksong made famous by Simon and Garfunkle, this juice is the ideal combination of vital force and calming influences. It's the gentle giant of Vitality Juices, since it nourishes body, mind and spirit. As a bonus, it also enhances memory, is cleansing and – thanks to the sage and thyme – is mildly antiseptic.

sage 6 leaves

carrots 4, unpeeled; unless organic, remove top and bottom

celery 3 sticks, with leaves

thyme leaves from 1 small sprig

parsley 1 handful, with stems

rosemary 2 teaspoons of leaves

vital statistics
Super-rich in **vitamin A** and **carotenoids**. Rich in **vitamin C** and **folic acid**. Contains **potassium**, **calcium** and small amounts of other **B vitamins**. The natural diuretic properties of celery and parsley give Scarborough Fair its cleansing properties, while the sage stimulates liver function, the rosemary improves memory and concentration and the thyme is a good antiseptic. This is an ideal choice for those dark autumn and winter mornings when you need help in getting both body and mind into gear.

papaya punch

It doesn't matter how good the food is that you eat; if it's not digested properly, it's of little benefit – a fact that Shakespeare, with his extraordinary perceptions of the human body and its frailties, knew only too well. 'Now, good digestion' says Macbeth in 'The Scottish Play', 'wait on appetite, and health on both!' The Bard would never have sampled a papaya, but he certainly would have approved of this Vitality Juice, which is both a stimulant of appetite and improver of digestion.

papaya 2 large, deseeded, flesh scooped out of skin
cantaloupe melon ½, peeled and deseeded
lime ½, peeled (unless key lime)
grapes 1 small bunch

vital statistics
Super-rich in **vitamins A** and **C** and **beta-carotene**. Rich in **potassium**. Contains **papain**, a powerful, protein-digesting enzyme that is especially effective on all meats. The tannins in the grape skins are an appetite stimulant, while cantaloupe is surprisingly rich in nutrients but also contains digestive enzymes. This combination generates maximum vitality through optimum digestion.

tutti-frutti

It's no coincidence that grapes are one of the most popular fruits to give to sick or convalescing people. They're uniquely nourishing, regenerating and strengthening. When combined with the protective constituents of peaches, kiwi fruit and strawberries – not to mention the extraordinary antioxidant powers of passionfruit and pomegranate – grapes make this one of the most powerful of all Vitality Juices.

strawberries 6 medium

kiwi fruit 2, unpeeled

passion fruit 2, seeds scooped out into juicer

peaches 2, stoned

pomegranate 1, seeds and pith scooped out into juicer

red grapes 175 g (6 oz)

vital statistics

Rich in **vitamins A** and **C**. Although rich in vitamins, this Superjuice is far more valuable for the **tannins**, **flavones**, **enzymes** and other essential **aromatic oils** it provides. Just one glass of Tutti-frutti contains the quintessential vitality-enhancing and life-protecting elements of Nature. So what are you waiting for? Down the hatch!

kohl slaw

Kohlrabi is a direct descendant of the ancient wild cabbage introduced to Germany from Italy during the Middle Ages. Sadly, its popularity has not spread far beyond its German borders, but this ugly-looking bulbous vegetable tastes like a mixture of turnips and cabbage with a dash of peppery radish thrown in. As a founder member of the brassica vegetables – along with cabbage, cauliflower, broccoli, Brussels sprouts and many others – it's a powerful booster of the immune system and protects against many forms of cancer.

carrots 3, unpeeled; unless organic, remove top and bottom
celery 1 stick, with leaves
kohlrabi 1 small, with leaves
fennel ½ bulb

vital statistics
Rich in **vitamins A** and **C** and **potassium**.
Kohl Slaw combines the liver-stimulating chemicals
in fennel with the diuretic properties of celery and the
anti-oestrogen indoles of kohlrabi. (Indoles are substances
which particularly protect women against hormone-linked
cancers.) Other nutrients lower the risks of stomach and
bowel cancers, too – which makes this the perfect drink
for toasting your health!

beet treat

Vitality depends on every cell in the body receiving its fair share of good nutrition. The only way this can happen is when nutrients are absorbed by the blood and carried throughout the circulatory system, where essential nutrients are made available to individual cells. If your blood is not in peak condition, it won't perform this function efficiently, and vitality flags. This Vitality Juice helps build better blood and provides essential ingredients for cell protection.

carrots 3, unpeeled; unless organic, remove top and bottom

apples 2, unpeeled, uncored and quartered

beetroot 1 small, unpeeled, with leaves

vital statistics

Super-rich in **vitamins A, C** and **E**. Rich in **vitamin B$_6$**, **folic acid** and **potassium**. Contains **iron, calcium** and **magnesium**. In traditional medicine, beetroot has long been regarded as a blood improver – with good reason, considering all the **nutrients** and **vitamins** it contains. That is precisely why, in Eastern Europe, beetroot juice is still used as part of the treatment for leukaemia.

spring clean tonic

After a long, hard winter of cold weather, dull days and dark mornings and evenings, vitality can reach its lowest ebb. If you haven't boosted yours with fresh juices, then now's the time to start. Decoke your sluggish system with this blood-purifying, body-cleansing and vitality-stimulating drink. Honestly, it tastes much better than it sounds!

carrots 3, unpeeled; unless organic, remove top and bottom

spring greens 1 large leaf

cucumber ½ medium

red pepper ¼, deseeded

watercress 1 generous handful

spinach 1 generous handful of leaves

vital statistics
Super-rich in **vitamin A** and **carotenoids**. Rich in **sulphur** and **vitamin C**. The Spring Clean Tonic is more important for its phytochemicals than its basic vitamins and minerals. Special **carotenoids** in spinach and spring greens protect the eyes against degenerative diseases and the extra beta-carotenes from red pepper and cucumber help revitalize skin and the mucous membranes of the nose and throat. A great boost for the immune system, this tonic raises your vitality quotient in time for spring.

octet con spirito

Introducing the ultimate Vitality Juice. These eight vegetables combine to boost immunity, stimulate the liver, activate the kidneys and build better blood. The Octet con Spirito also reduces blood pressure, lessens the likelihood of blood clots and revitalizes the libido. And you don't even have to recycle a can once you've drunk it down!

asparagus 3 spears

carrots 3 large, unpeeled; unless organic, remove top and bottom

radishes 3, with leaves

celery 2 sticks, with leaves

beetroot 1 small, unpeeled, with leaves

garlic 1 clove, peeled

spinach 1 handful of leaves

spring onion 1 medium

vital statistics

Super-rich in **beta-carotene** and **carotenoids**. Rich in **vitamin C**, **riboflavin** and **folic acid**. Contains **potassium** and **phosphorus**. As well as the nutritional benefits listed above, the Octet con Spirito offers a host of other health benefits. The natural substances in garlic lower cholesterol and are also antibacterial and antifungal. Asparagus is cleansing and diuretic, while spring onions and garlic both help ward off chest infections.

aphrodisiac juices

'Properly speaking, there are no aphrodisiacs capable of endowing those blind to life with sight,' said Napoleon's chef, Kurmonsky. 'But for those with poor eyesight in this matter, there are substances which can act as magnifying lenses.' Folklore is full of magic foods said to awaken that slumbering Greek goddess of love and beauty, Aphrodite. But is there any truth in these old wives' (or husbands') tales? Surprisingly, many of the traditional aphrodisiac foods are indeed rich in nutrients that are vital to sexual performance and fertility. Oysters, for example, are the great traditional aphrodisiac food for men; Casanova reputedly ate 70 a day! Yet while they are extremely rich in zinc, which is essential for sperm formation, they don't happen to juice too well. So eat your oysters (or feed them to your lover) in the usual way, but instead of washing them down with Champagne or other forms of alcohol, try any one of these delicious Aphrodisiac Juices. The nuts and seeds they contain are useful for zinc and selenium; asparagus for its vitamins A and E; wheat germ, bananas and avocados for vitamins B and E. The heady aroma of volatile oils in rosemary can jump-start the senses in many ways – as can the stimulating effects of hot spices. Amazing substances in chocolate do in fact generate feelings of euphoria – similar to the feelings experienced while being in love. These foods work equally well for women and men.

I don't guarantee that the juices in this chapter are the equivalent of Viagra™ in a glass, but their ingredients have a centuries-old aphrodisiac reputation and they certainly don't harbour any unwanted side effects. Most of them are quick and easy to make, and all are delicious.

Some recipes need a combination of juicing and blending. If you don't have a blender, you can use one of the hand-held 'wand' type processors, or (for most recipes) a whisk is almost as good. So if you want to give your romance an added edge, get juicing, and may Cupid watch over you!

eastern promise

This most potent of Aphrodisiac Juices has a history shrouded in the mists of time. The sacred fig tree of India has been worshipped for 5,000 years, and the Spartan athletes of ancient Greece were fed a diet rich in figs to improve their performance – and not just in the arena. Add the noblest of fruits (the grape), which is cooling and aphrodisiac in itself, plus the Oriental aroma of papaya, and you truly have an Aphrodisiac Juice that is filled with Eastern Promise.

fresh figs 2, large

papaya 1, deseeded, flesh scooped out of skin

black grapes 225 g (8 oz)

vital statistics
Super-rich in **vitamins A** and **C**. All three ingredients in Eastern Promise are bursting with volatile oils and hormone-stimulating properties. The high quantity of fruit sugars in this juice provide instant energy, while the digestion-improving enzymes from the papaya make it the ideal accompaniment to a meal when your planned dessert is, shall we say, more interesting than ice cream.

oriental magic

The aphrodisiac properties of ginger (*see opposite*) are reinforced in this recipe by coriander, one of the most ancient culinary and medicinal plants. Over the past 3,500 years, its use has spread from China and Egypt, through Asia, North Africa and into Europe, where it has been used as an aphrodisiac since the Middle Ages. A candlelit supper, a smouldering incense stick, a glass of Oriental Magic and a rug in front of the fire... well, need I say more?

pineapple ½, unpeeled, cut to fit juicer
ginger 15 g (½ oz) fresh root, peeled and sliced
coriander 1 small bunch

vital statistics
Super-rich in **vitamin C**. Rich in **potassium**. Full of healing and stimulating enzymes, Oriental Magic gets its punch from the volatile oils of ginger and the flavonoids, cumarins and other plant chemicals found in coriander. The contrasting flavours of pineapple and ginger, together with the powerful phytochemicals present in coriander, give this juice a surprising but nonetheless delicious flavour.

ginger up juice

Ginger is a vital ingredient in ancient Chinese medicine and the traditional Ayurvedic healing of India. As well as its powerful medicinal actions, ginger is immensely stimulating. When we use the expression 'ginger someone up', we're invoking the genuine properties of this wonderful root. Combined with the cooling, energising properties of watermelon, this is one of the simplest yet most effective Aphrodisiac Juices.

ginger 25 g (1 oz), fresh root, peeled and sliced
watermelon ¼ large, with seeds and skin

vital statistics
Contains small amounts of **vitamins A**, **C** and **E**. Ginger Up Juice is not included in this book purely for its nutritional value. It does contain traces of vitamins, but these are not significant; its enzymes and gentle diuretic substances are its true assets. Ginger contains substances called **gingerol** and **zingiberene**, which dilate the blood vessels and improve circulation – vital for male sexual performance, but equally important for female enjoyment.

cherry ripe

Don't be fooled by the seemingly innocent ingredients in Cherry Ripe: its effects can be powerful and rapid. The sensuous aroma of strawberries, combined with the sweet, heady taste of cherry juice, makes this simple recipe extra special. As a bonus, the natural aspirin-like substances found in strawberries make Cherry Ripe a particularly good juice for anyone with unwanted aches and pains who's planning a night of passion.

strawberries 450 g (1 lb)
cherries 225 g (8 oz), stoned

vital statistics

Super-rich in **vitamin C**. Rich in **bioflavonoids** and **vitamin A**. Contains **calcium, potassium, folic acid, B vitamins** and some **magnesium**.

In addition to stimulating the senses, this Aphrodisiac Juice helps neutralize uric acid – that is why it's so helpful for those with rheumatism, arthritis or even gout. The volatile oils produce a heady perfume that is at once sensuous and arousing – which makes removing all those cherry stones well worth the effort!

sweet surrender

Bananas are credited with aphrodisiac powers in the folklore of many countries, but don't eat them until they're fully ripe – that is to say, when the skins are completely yellow and starting to mottle with brown specks. In Asia and the Middle East, honey is regarded as a great aphrodisiac. This delicious and refreshing smoothie combines all the enzyme and energizing benefits of watermelon with the staying power of bananas. To make it, juice the watermelon, then combine with the ice cubes, honey, yogurt and banana in a blender.

watermelon ¼, with seeds and skin; cut to fit juicer
banana 1, peeled
live yogurt 125 g (4½ oz), plain
honey 1 teaspoon
ice cubes 1 handful

vital statistics
Rich in **calcium**, **potassium**, **vitamins A, C and E**, and **chromium**. The potassium in bananas is great for lovers, since it fosters prolonged muscular effort without cramp. Bananas are also one of the very few fruits containing chromium, a mineral essential for energy metabolism and sexual function. The instant energy from the honey and banana will give your love life a helpful kick-start, too!

hot and juicy

In the traditional Ayurvedic medicine of India – home of the fabled *Kama Sutra* – the pumpkin is believed to both preserve and increase male virility. In Hot and Juicy, its cool, health-giving juice is combined deliciously with the distinctive flavour of apple and the unusual, slightly nutty taste of lamb's lettuce. The sting in the tail comes from the red chilli – so be prepared for fireworks!

apple 1, unpeeled, uncored and quartered
pumpkin 350 g (12 oz), peeled
red chilli ½ small, deseeded
lamb's lettuce 1 handful

vital statistics
Rich in **vitamins A** and **C**. Contains some **B vitamins**, **folic acid** and **potassium**. The plant chemicals in pumpkin have a gentle aphrodisiac effect, but it's the capsaicin in the chilli pepper that is a remarkable circulatory stimulant. It has a dramatic effect on blood flow and male potency. A glass at bedtime should almost guarantee a hot and juicy night.

femme fatale

Unless you have North African or Arabic friends, or have travelled to these parts of the world, you may never have heard of, let alone tasted, purslane. But it has been used as a medicinal plant since Roman times, and eaten as a vegetable long before that. It's one of the few plant sources of omega-3 fatty acids – and these are the ingredients that make it a mood-enhancing food for women. You should be able to find it in ethnic shops which stock African or Moroccan foods.

sweet apples 4, unpeeled, uncored and quartered
radishes 4 medium
purslane 225 g (8 oz)
alfalfa sprouts 1 handful

vital statistics
Rich in **vitamins A** and **C**. Contains some **calcium** and **B vitamins**. Femme Fatale gets a hefty shot of phytoestrogens from the radishes, sensuous volatile oils from apples and calming B vitamins from alfalfa sprouts. Add the essential fatty acids and bladder-calming substances derived from the purslane, and this is just the juice to trigger a fatal attraction.

passionate pumpkin

It's the tiny pinch of saffron that adds the vibrant colour tones to this already bright-yellow delectable juice. Certainly the most expensive spice in the world – it takes more than 20,000 hand-picked stigmas and styles from the saffron crocus to make 115 g (4 oz) – saffron is also highly prized for its aphrodisiac properties. Used in ancient India, Greece and Rome, it was also reputed by medieval herbalists to quicken the spirit and heart.

apricots 2, stoned

mango 1, peeled and stoned

pumpkin 1 slice, peeled

Juice the above, then combine with the ingredients below in a blender.

wheat germ 1 dessertspoon

sesame seeds 1 teaspoon

saffron 1 tiny pinch

ice cubes 1 handful

vital statistics
Super-rich in **vitamins A, C** and **carotenoids**. Rich in **vitamin E, B vitamins** and **zinc**. Passionate Pumpkin makes a potent remedy for both sexes which also encourages the production of healthy sperm; what's more, it makes a perfect drink at any time of the day. The volatile constituents from saffron also help soothe menstrual cramps and pain.

french kicker

Garlic as an aphrodisiac? *Mais oui!* After all, 50 million Frenchmen can't be wrong. Combined with a selection of colourful salad leaves (make sure you add plenty of the red and darker-coloured ones), this juice is both a sexual stimulant and has a calming effect on the mind. Hence, it takes away all those anxieties that so commonly lead to poor performance.

carrots 2, unpeeled; unless organic, remove top and bottom

garlic 1 clove, peeled

lime 1, with peel

salad leaves mixed, 350 g (12 oz)

vital statistics

Rich in **vitamins A**, **C** and **E**. Contains **chlorophyll**, **magnesium**, **potassium** and **silicon**. As a bonus, the French Kicker is a really good hair tonic – but you're not thinking about that now! Just enjoy the calming natural opiates in the lettuce, the stimulating sulphur compounds in the garlic and the **bioflavonoids** in the lime that strengthen the circulatory system. It's enough to make anyone say *ooh la la!*

mountain rescue

Swiss chard may seem an unlikely contender to include in an
Aphrodisiac Juice, but it's rich in nutrients and you can juice the
leaf as well as the fleshy stalk. In case you feel like serenading
your partner, leeks are good for the voice – the Roman emperor
Nero ate some every day to improve his – but they're also a
soothing nerve tonic.

swiss chard 4 leaves

leek 7.5 cm (3 inches)

apples 3, unpeeled, uncored and quartered

asparagus 2 spears

celery 2 sticks, with leaves

vital statistics
Super-rich in **vitamins A, C** and **folic acid**. Rich
in **carotenoids** and **potassium**. Contains **iron**
and some **vitamin E**. Mountain Rescue is a valuable
aphrodisiac tonic for late-summer/early autumn – an ideal
way to get ready for those long, snowy winters! The folic
acid and vitamin E it contains provide vital stimulants,
while the sulphur compounds in leeks help reduce
cholesterol and improve blood flow.

bunnies' bonanza

If you really want to find out whether it's true what they say about rabbits, just try a glass of Bunnies' Bonanza. The traditional aphrodisiac benefits of coriander and celery, the sexual stimulants in parsley and the plant oestrogens in cabbage make this the perfect potion for couples.

carrots 3, unpeeled; unless organic, remove top and bottom

cabbage 2 dark-green leaves

celery 1 stick, with leaves

coriander 1 handful

parsley 1 handful, with stems

vital statistics
Super-rich in **vitamins A** and **C**. Rich in **sulphur**. Contains some **calcium** and **iron**. It's the phytochemicals that work in this mixture. The potent volatile oils in coriander and celery, and the strengthening indoles in cabbage are the key – which is probably why cabbage is known as the medicine of the poor throughout Europe. The antiviral benefit of carrots and the anti-bacterial properties of coriander also make sure there'll be no bugs in your bunny.

asparadisia

There are pictures of cultivated asparagus in 6,000-year-old Egyptian tombs, and it has been used medicinally ever since. Whether its reputation as an aphrodisiac comes merely from its shape or from its chemical constituents is unclear, but it has been accorded this attribute by civilizations throughout the world. Combined here with the fortifying strength of broccoli and watercress, this is the most health-giving of drinks.

asparagus 6 spears

carrots 2, unpeeled; unless organic, remove top and bottom

broccoli 1 head, florets only

watercress 1 handful

vital statistics

Super-rich in **vitamins A**, **C** and **folic acid** and **potassium**. Contains **iron**, **calcium** and **phosphorous**. Surprisingly, asparagus contains substantial amounts of protein for a vegetable – as much, in fact, as the same weight of rice, corn on the cob or a bean and vegetable casserole. The slow-release energy from this protein and the combined constituents of the other vegetables make Asparadisia your gateway to paradise.

pick-me-up juices

Even in the best-ordered lives there are times when hauling yourself out of bed requires a superhuman effort. There are days when energy seems so lacking that the thought of getting dressed and dragging yourself to work is enough to bring on an instant attack of doom and gloom. I call this TTFN (Total but Temporary Fatigue Neurosis), and 75 per cent of the population say they wake up with it at some time. Of course, the more common causes of TTFN are self-inflicted: too much booze the night before; burning the candle at both ends; an endless diet of junk food, sticky buns and sweets. Yet many people suffer TTFN through no fault of their own. They are simply ground down by the stresses and pressures of modern life, jobs and children; illness or infection; poor absorption of nutrients due to digestive problems; or other physical disorders such as Seasonal Affective Disorder (SAD), ME or chronic fatigue syndrome. Even in the absence of all these problems, however, nutritional deficiencies are frequently the cause of TTFN. Intensively grown crops raised on poor soil, intensively farmed animals reared in far-from-ideal circumstances, even apparently good food so processed that it loses substantial amounts of its original value... all of these things eventually take their toll.

One universally ignored cause of TTFN is the depletion of nutrients and other vital substances that results from long-term use of prescribed and over-the-counter medicines. Many doctors are unaware of the damaging effects some medicines have on nutritional wellbeing (see Chemical Robbery, page 149).

These are just some of the reasons why so many people need a pick me up, and there's no better way to get one than with a glass of freshly made juice. For extra potency, some of the juices in this section are fortified by the addition of such power-packing nutrients as wheat germ, molasses, nuts and seeds, dried fruits, maple syrup, honey, soya milk, tofu, kelp and vitamins.

c-plus

C-plus is just the thing to boost your natural resistance and give you that extra 'get up and go' if you're feeling a bit more than one degree under par. Echinacea is a plant that is native to North America but now grows widely throughout Europe. It has been used for centuries by herbalists for its ability to support and enhance the body's own immune system. To create this Pick-me-up Juice, use a 1000 mg soluble vitamin C tablet, dissolve it in a little water, add the echinacea extract, stir into the finished juice and drink immediately. You can find both the vitamin C tablets and echinacea at chemists or good health-food stores.

oranges 2, peeled, but leaving pith on

*grapefruit 1, peeled, but leaving pith on

key lime 1, unpeeled

vitamin c 1000 mg tablet

echinacea extract 30 drops

*If taking prescribed medicines, consult your doctor before drinking large amounts of grapefruit juice.

vital statistics
Doubly Super-rich in **vitamin C**: a glass of C-plus is equivalent to a whole week's requirement. The abundant **bioflavonoids** from the citrus fruits make this juice a superb free-radical scavenger which cleans up the system and provides excellent Superjuice protection.

super stinger

Make sure you wear gloves when gathering the stinging nettles, but don't worry – the juice won't sting. Nettles have been used as a medicine since the earliest times and were one of the favourite herbs of the first-century Greek physician Dioscorides. This powerful herb, combined with the immune-boosting benefits of carrots and spinach, makes this an instant tonic.

carrots 3, unpeeled; unless organic, remove top and bottom

apples 2, unpeeled, uncored and quartered

stinging nettles 1 bunch young, pale-green

spinach 1 handful of leaves

vital statistics
Super-rich in **vitamin A**. Rich in **vitamin C**. Contains calcium, **potassium** and **iron**. The flavonoids in spinach and nettles boost Super Stinger's protective value, while the vitamin C from the apples improves absorption of its iron content. This is an ideal juice for nursing mothers as it increases the flow of breast milk, guards against anaemia and restores energy.

stir-fry starter

Here is everything you get in an Oriental restaurant, without the wok. Like our home-grown savoy cabbage, these exotic relatives – Chinese cabbage and Pak Choi – are members of the *Cruciferae* family. Their flavours blend perfectly with those of carrots and sweet potato. The rich mineral content of seaweed is a vital addition to this recipe, while sesame seeds supply both energy and that elusive Oriental flavour. Anyone suffering or recovering from serious illness will benefit from this powerful pick me up. Sprinkle the sesame seeds onto the finished juice for a massive energy, vitamin and mineral bonus.

carrots 2, unpeeled; unless organic, remove top and bottom
sweet potato 1 small, unpeeled
chinese cabbage ½ medium
pak choi 1 handful
seaweed 1 handful (wash to remove salt)
sesame seeds 2 teaspoons

vital statistics
Super-rich in **vitamins A, C, E, carotenoids, folic acid** and **potassium**. Contains some **B vitamins, iron, magnesium** and **iodine**. This juice is bursting with the **phytochemicals** which encourage detoxification, work against hormone-related cancers and protect against cell damage in general. Hence, Stir-fry Starter is ideal for anyone suffering from ME, chronic fatigue, overwork or just plain tiredness.

entente cordiale

This combination of the typically British carrot and beetroot with the sunny Mediterranean taste of fresh basil leaves combines the best of northern and southern European flavours. The blood-building benefits of beetroot contrast delightfully with the cooling flavour of cucumber, while the energy-giving natural sugars in the root vegetables blend wonderfully with the heady aroma, digestive benefits and mentally stimulating effects of basil.

carrots 3, unpeeled; unless organic, remove top and bottom

beetroot 1 medium, unpeeled, with leaves

cucumber ½ medium

basil 1 handful of leaves

vital statistics
Super-rich in **vitamin A**. Rich in **folic acid** and **potassium**. Contains **vitamin C**, **magnesium** and **calcium**. It isn't just the obvious protective nutrients that make this juice a pick me up, but the betaine (an anthocyanin) in beetroot, which improves the quality of the blood. Like so many herbs, basil has an ancient history as a medicine and, whether taken in this juice or used in cooking, it energizes both mind and body.

welsh ginger

Is it coincidence that one of the national symbols of Wales is the leek? The Welsh are renowned for their wonderful choirs – and leeks have been used to soothe, protect and improve the quality of the voice since Roman times. Even so, it's not for its vocal properties that the leek is combined here with carrots, parsley and ginger. Like its close relatives, garlic and onions, the leek boosts immunity and stimulates energy. Combined with the ginger, it makes this a guaranteed pep-up recipe.

carrots 4, unpeeled; unless organic, remove top and bottom

leek 1 small

parsley 1 handful, with stems

ginger 15 g (½ oz) fresh root, peeled and sliced

vital statistics
Super-rich in **vitamin A**, **beta-carotene** and other vital **carotenoids**. Rich in **potassium**. Contains **vitamin C** and **calcium**. The **phytochemicals** in the leek stimulate good digestion and improve nutrient absorption to increase energy levels. The gentle diuretic effects of parsley help eliminate toxins (especially after illness), while the ginger stimulates circulation and perks up the entire system.

life saver

Just the juice to revive that sinking feeling! Of all the lettuces, iceberg probably has the least amount of nutrients – especially when compared with the dark-green and red-leaved varieties. However, it doesn't go slimy in your fridge after three days; in fact, it will keep well for two weeks if wrapped in clingfilm. It has a much sweeter flavour than other types of lettuce and contains the highest levels of natural calming substances. If you're tense, anxious and irritable, or run down, then this juice is the cure for you.

apples 3, unpeeled, uncored and quartered
oranges 2, peeled, but leaving pith on
lemon 1, with peel if thin-skinned
iceberg lettuce 2 handfuls

vital statistics
Super-rich in **vitamin C** and **folic acid**. Contains **vitamin A**, **iron**, **calcium** and masses of **potassium**. This Superjuice is also a good source of protective **flavonoids**. Lettuce contains substances known as **lactones**, and was used by the ancient Assyrians as a mild sedative. All of these properties make the Life Saver an ideal calming and restorative juice for children recovering from illness.

peppery pick-up

The instant energy from the molasses and the natural sugars in the apricots work hand-in-hand with the beneficial constituents of the other ingredients in this delicious and stimulating cooler. The liver-activating properties of fennel stimulate the detoxifying process, while the cleansing effects of the peppers will soon get you back on your feet.

oranges 2, peeled, but leaving pith on

fennel 1 medium bulb

red pepper ½, deseeded

yellow pepper ½, deseeded

Juice the above, then combine with the ingredients below in a blender.

dried apricots 4, soaked overnight

molasses 1 dessertspoon

ice cubes 1 handful

vital statistics
Super-rich in **vitamins A** and **C**, **carotenoids**, **potassium**. Contains **calcium**, **magnesium**, **phosphorus** and **iron**. Peppery Pick-up is especially healing to the stomach thanks to the fennel. The massive carotenoid content in this juice is a sure-fire recipe for rapid recovery. Its calcium, magnesium and potassium content also make it a great tonic after strenuous physical exercise.

buzz juice

In this recipe, the tropical fruits alone would make a truly wonderful Pick-me-up Juice, but once you add guarana, you'll be buzzing. The Rain Forest Indians in Brazil discovered guarana, and I've learned what a wonderful energy-giver this strange berry can be. Guarana isn't a quick shot in the arm and a let-down half an hour later; it supplies a slow release of energy over several hours (you can find guarana extract in most good health-food shops). To make Buzz Juice, juice all the fruits except the banana (look for mangosteens in supermarkets in season), then liquidize with the banana, guarana extract and ice cubes. Drink immediately.

mango 1, peeled, without stone

guava 1, peeled

passionfruit 1, flesh scooped out into juicer

mangosteen 1, cut in half, flesh scooped into juicer

banana 1, peeled

guarana extract 1 tablespoon

ice cubes 1 handful

vital statistics
Super-rich in **vitamin C**, **carotenoids** and **potassium**. Contains **B vitamins** and **folic acid**. All the tropical fruits supply **antioxidants** and are highly protective, but they also contain an abundance of natural **enzymes**. These substances speed up the healing process after surgery or injury; they also stimulate the immune system, and some are involved in the conversion of carbohydrates into usable energy for the body. It's impossible to feel low for long once you start to get the buzz from this unique and beautifully flavoured drink.

on your mark

If you're putting off exercise because you just can't work up enough enthusiasm, this is the juice for you. On Your Mark is perfect before a round of golf, a game of tennis, an evening of ten-pin bowling, a session in the gym, a cycle ride or even just a long, brisk walk. The slow-release energy from the parsnip and carrots, the instant fruit sugars in the tangerines, and the sustaining benefits of the apple will certainly get you on your mark and raring to go.

tangerines 4, peeled

carrots 2, unpeeled; unless organic, remove top and bottom

apple 1, unpeeled, uncored and quartered

parsnip 1 large, unpeeled

vital statistics
Super-rich in **vitamin C** and **beta-carotene**. Rich in **potassium**, **phosphorus**, **sulphur** and **silicon**. Contains **vitamin E** and some **B vitamins**. The complex starches in the parsnip and carrots break down slowly, providing a gradual release of energy that is ideal for sporting activities. This juice will give you an instant lift and get you in the right frame of mind and body to enjoy any sporting interests.

ready, steady, go

If you've used On Your Mark (see opposite) and it's given you enough of a boost to start thinking about exercise, then this is the juice to really get you up and going. It combines masses of energy from the pears, kiwi fruit and wheat germ with the super-protection against free radicals derived from the watercress and the soya yogurt. This is the ideal regular juice when you're feeling a bit down but really want to be more active. It's great for everyone but particularly good for women, as soya helps control hormone fluctuations.

pears 2, unpeeled
kiwi fruit 1, unpeeled
broccoli 115 g (4 oz), florets only
soya yogurt 125 g (4¼ oz)
wheat germ 2 tablespoons
watercress 1 bunch

vital statistics
Super-rich in **vitamin C**. Rich in **beta-carotene** and **carotenoids**. Contains **iron**, **sulphur**, **vitamin E** and **protein**. As well as the generally protective benefits of all the carotenoids and the vitamin C, this juice is rich in **phytochemicals** from the broccoli and the watercress which are extremely important for the protection of lung tissue against cancer. The vitamin E in wheat germ helps the circulation and will keep you ahead of the field no matter what your chosen sport.

pick-me-up juices   93

wake-up whammy

Here's a Pick-me-up Juice with a vengeance. Make sure you choose the ripest possible tomatoes, as that's when they're at their most nutritious. Most people don't realize that tomatoes are a member of the *Solanaceae* family, which includes potatoes, peppers and aubergines; they're all relatives of the nightshade. For this reason, this juice is not ideal for anyone with rheumatoid arthritis, though it's not a problem if you have osteoarthritis. To make it, stir the kelp powder (you can find it in most good health-food shops) into the juice just before drinking.

tomatoes 4 medium

sweet potato 1 small, unpeeled

ginger 25 g (1 oz) fresh root, peeled and sliced

celery 2 sticks, with leaves

kelp powder 2 teaspoons

vital statistics
Super-rich in **vitamin C**, **beta-carotene**, **lycopene** and **iodine**. Contains **potassium** and **folic acid**. As well as all the protective benefits of the **carotenoids** and vitamin C, this juice also contains some coumarin compounds from the celery which pep up the entire circulatory system, boost the protective function of white cells and lower blood pressure. The kelp powder is rich in iodine, which stimulates the thyroid and gets your body working in overdrive.

grapefruit glitz

When peeling the grapefruit and oranges to make this fruit-packed Superjuice, be sure to leave plenty of the white pith still attached to the flesh, as this is where this tonic's bioflavonoids are found. If you're lucky enough to find very thin-skinned lemons, there's no need to peel them at all – although it's best to taste a little of the peel first, as this can sometimes be very bitter.

*grapefruit 2, peeled, but leaving pith on

oranges 2, peeled, but leaving pith on

lemon 1, with peel if thin-skinned

*If taking prescribed medicines, consult your doctor before drinking large amounts of grapefruit juice.

vital statistics
Super-rich in **vitamin C** and **potassium**.
Contains useful amounts of **calcium**. It's not just the vitamin C content that is so important in this recipe, it's the wide range of protective **flavonoids** which helps increase natural immunity against both bacteria and viruses, and plays a major part in protecting the body against cancer. As a bonus, you'll also get a substantial shot of **folic acid** and some useful **vitamin A**.

protective juices

The human body should survive in an active, healthy state for 120 years, but as most of us know, it rarely does. However, in parts of the world where longevity is taken for granted – by the Hunza tribesmen in the Himalayas, the Lamas of Tibet, the Fakirs of India – diets are rich in nuts, berries, fruits and fermented milk products. Today we all have access to the concentrated protective power of these natural foods in the form of Protective Juices.

Many years ago, I spent a few days working with one of the most famous nutritional healers of modern times, Gayelord Hauser, who numbered most of the great Hollywood stars of the Forties, Fifties and Sixties among his clients. He was convinced that a daily pint of fresh juice was the best safeguard against illness and premature ageing.

Certainly, the vegetables and fruits that go into such juices contain a protective anti-cancer cocktail we cannot afford to ignore. Tragically, however, during a typical week, three-quarters of adults don't eat a single piece of citrus fruit, half of them don't eat an apple or a pear, and two-thirds don't touch any type of green vegetable. For maximum protection against cancer as well as general health benefits, we should all eat a wide variety of fresh produce and drink at least one glass of fresh juice daily.

Everyone knows that fruits, salads and vegetables contain vitamins and minerals, but few are aware of their powerful protective constituents. Natural plant substances known as phytochemicals play a major part in the protective action of these foods against cancers and other diseases, and they do so in a variety of ways. Carrots and green vegetables, for example, protect against lung cancer, while it has been shown that increased consumption of fruit lowers the risk of mouth and throat cancers.

The Protective Juices in this chapter allow you to create your own glassful of these and other vital cancer fighters. Incorporated as a regular part of your health regime, the following recipes could literally protect your life.

long-life lemonade

Sauerkraut might sound like a strange thing to juice, but this pickled cabbage is used as a traditional East European protective medicine against stomach ulcers and cancer. Combined with the cancer-fighting properties of beetroot and carrots, as well the apple's natural pectin fibre (which protects the heart and circulation), it makes this juice very special. It tastes much better than it sounds, too, since the sauerkraut's slightly acidic flavour is offset by the sweetness of the other ingredients.

carrots 3, unpeeled; unless organic, remove top and bottom

radishes 3 medium, with leaves

apples 2, unpeeled, uncored and quartered

lemon 1, with peel if thin-skinned

beetroot 1 medium, unpeeled with leaves

sauerkraut 2 tablespoons

vital statistics
Super-rich in **beta-carotene**, **vitamin C**, **potassium** and **folic acid**. Contains **calcium** and **iron**. The massive potassium content of beetroot with its leaves helps keep blood pressure low – vital for a long and active life. The radishes are specifically healing to the mucous membranes of the nose, sinuses and throat while protecting against chest infections.

cucumber soother

This Protective Juice helps to prevent as well as cure sore throats, tonsillitis, laryngitis and sinusitis. How? Well, the healing properties of carrots combine well with the soothing effect of cucumber on the mucous membranes, and the diuretic action of celery reduces swelling of the tonsils, adenoids and throat. Add sage, which is powerfully antiseptic and a traditional remedy for all mouth and throat problems, and you have some real ammunition against the woes of winter.

carrots 3, unpeeled; unless organic, remove top and bottom
celery 2 sticks, with leaves
pineapple 1 small
sage 6 fresh leaves
cucumber 15 cm (6 in)

vital statistics
Super-rich in **beta-carotene**, **potassium** and **natural enzymes**. Contains **vitamin C** and **folic acid**. The natural enzyme **bromelain** in pineapple is especially healing to the lining of the mouth and throat; it is also a great aid to digestion, so it maximizes the extraction of nutrients from foods. Sage is a valuable antiseptic due to its high content of the essential oil known as **thujone**.

savoir vivre

You'll get super-power protection from this recipe. The combined properties of garlic and ginger for heart and circulation, the infection-fighting benefits of the artichoke, and the general immune benefits of melon and chicory make this Superjuice one of the best all-round protectors there is.

carrots 3, unpeeled; unless organic, remove top and bottom

jerusalem artichokes 2, unpeeled, well scrubbed

garlic 1 clove, peeled

chicory 1 small head

melon ½ small yellow, deseeded, sliced, with skin

ginger 15 g (½ oz) fresh root, peeled and sliced

vital statistics
Super-rich in **vitamins A**, **C**, **folic acid** and **potassium**. Contains **iron**, **magnesium**, **calcium**, some **vitamin E** and **B vitamins**. Nothing could be better than Savoir Vivre as a regular once-a-week boost to the immune system. Its high vitamin C content allows the minerals to be much more easily absorbed, and the volatile oils in ginger and garlic are key factors in protecting against heart and circulatory disease.

dracula's delight

Just the juice to protect your blood and your immune system. Though Dracula is supposed to dislike garlic, it is certainly one of the most powerful of blood purifiers. At times of stress – physical or mental – the immune system is likely to suffer, leaving you prey to all sorts of marauding bugs. Dracula's Delight is the tonic you need at these times, but it's also good as a regular dose of health insurance, especially during the winter months.

apples 4, unpeeled, uncored and quartered
celery 2 sticks, with leaves
garlic 2 cloves, peeled

vital statistics
Rich in **potassium** and **vitamin C**. The real value of this Protective Juice lies in the **phytochemicals** it contains. **Ellagic acid** from the apples has powerful anti-cancer qualities, while coumarins in the celery also protect against cancer, reduce blood pressure and act as a tonic to the circulatory system. Combined with the antifungal, anti-bacterial and heart-protective substances in garlic, they make for an excellent glassful of protection.

good mouthkeeping

More people lose their teeth through gum disease than tooth decay. Naturally, there's no substitute for proper mouth care and regular visits to your dentist and hygienist. However, smoking, alcohol and very hot drinks can all damage the delicate tissues inside the mouth and throat – which is why this juice is designed specifically to protect those sensitive areas.

radishes 6, with leaves

carrots 4, unpeeled; unless organic, remove top and bottom

tomatoes 4 medium, ripe

spring onion 1 medium

leek 15 cm (6 in), cut lengthways in strips

Optional: Worcestershire sauce and freshly ground black pepper to taste

vital statistics
Super-rich in **vitamins A**, **C** and **carotenoids**. Contains **folic acid**, **potassium** and some **calcium**. The very high vitamin A content in carrots and tomatoes, together with the wide selection of other **carotenoids** and **lycopenes**, offer specific protection against cancers of the mouth and throat. The sulphur content in radishes is anti-bacterial and their bitter flavour stimulates the flow of saliva – which is crucial to the prevention of gum disease.

pro-bonus 1

The earlier women start to build healthy bones, the less likely they are to develop osteoporosis in later life. The Superjuices Pro-bonus 1 and 2 are good sources of easily absorbed calcium and magnesium, both of which are essential for bone development. They're a great bone tonic for women throughout life – but don't forget that some men also develop osteoporosis, so it's good for them, too.

apples 3, unpeeled, uncored and quartered

celery 2 sticks, with leaves

beetroot 1 medium, unpeeled with leaves

cabbage ½ small round, cut in wedges

vital statistics
Super-rich in **calcium**, **magnesium** and **vitamin C**. Rich in **folic acid** and **potassium**. Contains **iron** and **phosphorus**. The extra nutrients from the beet tops, the cancer-fighting bonus of the nutrients in cabbage and the calming influences of celery make this Protective Juice a powerful tonic as well as a bone builder.

pro-bonus 2

This juice is not so rich in calcium as Pro-bonus 1, but it is a treasure trove of other micronutrients that are vital for the formation of healthy bones. Pro-bonus 2 is ideal at any age, but it is especially good for women approaching, going through or after the menopause, as it ensures the best utilization of other calcium sources in the diet.

carrots 4, unpeeled; unless organic, remove top and bottom

chard leaves 3 large, with stalks

apples 2, unpeeled, uncored and quartered

broccoli 2 stems of purple sprouting variety, with leaves

red pepper 1 small, deseeded and quartered

watercress 1 handful, with stalks

vital statistics
Super-rich in **vitamins A, C, E, B$_6$, folic acid, potassium** and **magnesium**. Contains **vitamin K, calcium, boron**, some other **B vitamins** and **iron**. Consuming large quantities of calcium will not, on its own, help your body form and maintain strong and healthy bones. It's vital to include the trace minerals and vitamins that are essential to this complex process – and this Superjuice has an abundance of them all.

soy salsa

If this drink were a drug, it would be hailed as 'a breakthrough' by the pharmaceutical industry! Its heart and artery-protecting traits combine the kick of a Mexican mule with the cancer-fighting properties of the soya bean; for those with a delicate digestion, there are also the stomach-soothing benefits of mint. Soy Salsa also guards against joint damage and chest infections. To make this drink, stir the soya milk into the finished juice.

mint 6 leaves

spring onions 2 medium

tomatoes 2 medium

jalapeño pepper 1 small, deseeded

garlic 1 clove, peeled

cucumber ½ medium

soya milk 125 ml (4 fl oz)

vital statistics

Rich in **vitamin A**. Contains **vitamin C**, **potassium** and **folic acid**. Here's another Superjuice that is more valuable for its **phytochemicals** than for its vitamin and mineral content. Jalapeño peppers, tomatoes, garlic, spring onions, mint and soya milk contain (respectively) substances which protect against joint disease, heart disease, bacterial and fungal infections, high blood pressure, digestive upsets and breast cancer. What more could you ask?

skin deep

Helena Rubenstein once said, 'Never put anything on your face that you wouldn't put in your mouth.' Well, this juice is far too good to waste on the outside, as it's not only a skin healer and cleanser but a powerful skin protector. Beauty is definitely more than skin deep, and it's pointless wasting time and money on lotions and potions if you're not feeding the skin with everything it needs from within.

carrots 4, unpeeled; unless organic, remove top and bottom

asparagus 2 spears

iceberg lettuce ½ medium

spinach 1 handful of leaves

vital statistics
Super-rich in **vitamins A** and **C**, **beta-carotene** and **folic acid**. Rich in **iron** and **vitamin E**. Contains **potassium**, **silica** and some **B vitamins**. Not only does it protect against skin infections, thanks to its high vitamin A and beta-carotene content, Skin Deep also provides plenty of vitamin E, which helps maintain supple and wrinkle-free skin. This juice is also a blood builder – which means more skin nutrients are carried to the surface where they're needed.

back to school

Put the fruit juice in a blender with the banana, yogurt, honey and echinacea to make this great immune booster. It's terrific at any time, but give your children an extra three glasses of this juice in the week before they go back to school. They're going to come into contact with all sorts of bugs they haven't encountered during the holidays or before starting school. This Superjuice offers protection against bacteria and viruses, and will help keep them illness-free. By the way: it works for parents, too!

tangerines 3 (or satsumas or clementines), peeled

pineapple ½, unpeeled, sliced

blackcurrants 115 g (4 oz), fresh or frozen

banana 1, peeled

yogurt 125 g (4½ oz), live

runny honey 1 dessertspoon

echinacea 10 drops herbal extract

vital statistics
Super-rich in **vitamin C**, **bioflavonoids**, **potassium**, beneficial live bacteria and healthy calories. The dark-coloured **pigments** in blackcurrants give a healthy boost to the body's own natural defences as well as protection against some cancers. The live beneficial **bacteria** from the yogurt not only ensure good digestion, but are also known to play a vital part in the immune process.

eye brite

In these days of computers, VDUs and TV watching, it has become more important to protect the eyes. The most common cause of poor sight and blindness in elderly people is Age-related Macular Degeneration, or AMD. The latest evidence shows that this disease tends to coincide with a low intake of specific carotenoids. People who consistently eat foods containing these protective substances are at much lower risk of getting AMD.

carrots 4, unpeeled; unless organic, remove top and bottom

kale 2 leaves

watercress 1 bunch

parsley 1 small handful, with stems

spinach 1 handful of leaves

vital statistics
Super-rich in **vitamin A**, **beta-carotene** and other essential **carotenoids**. Contains **vitamins C** and **E**, **folic acid** and **iron**. The old wives' tale that carrots help you see in the dark is true. Beta-carotene is essential for proper night vision, and other carotenoids, such as **lutein** and **xeaxanthine** in spinach and kale, also protect against AMD (see above). This is a juice to drink regularly for long-term eye health and protection.

doctor garlic

This Superjuice may not win friends and influence people, and it is not for the faint-hearted, but Doctor Garlic represents the ultimate in veggie power. This Superjuice exploits the pick of the protective vegetables with the kick of garlic, mooli and jalapeño. An all-year-round immune booster with massive built-in protection, it tastes seriously better than it sounds – but make sure you drink it with the one you love.

garlic 3 cloves, peeled

carrots 2, unpeeled; unless organic, remove top and bottom

celery 1 stick, with leaves

tomato 1 medium, ripe

sweet potato 1, scrubbed, unpeeled, cut into sticks

jalapeño pepper ½, deseeded

mooli (white radish) 7.5 cm (3 in)

vital statistics
Super-rich in **vitamins A, C, E, carotenoids** and **potassium**. Rich in **B₆, folic acid, magnesium, iron,** and other **B vitamins**. This is a meal in a glass, but it's not just the conventional nutrients which make Doctor Garlic so valuable. The enormous protective benefits of garlic cover heart, circulation, chest infections, other bacteria and fungi. Ginger also protects the heart and, together with the jalapeño pepper, the joints, too. Mooli, the white radish, is one of the great liver protectors.

booze juices

Since ancient times, man has made alcoholic drinks, from the most primitive fermented beer to wine and distilled spirits. Alcohol has played a major part in religious ceremonies, has been used medicinally and for celebration, but few things have polarized views as much as the arguments for and against the plain enjoyment of booze.

In Victorian times, anti-alcohol campaigners battled against 'demon drink' – so much so, in fact, that Victorian women perpetuated the myth that eating cheese late at night caused nightmares in order to stop their menfolk drinking the port that went with the Stilton. In the US, Prohibition proved to be a disaster as well as a failure – it certainly didn't stop anybody from drinking if they wanted to do so.

So what is the truth about alcohol? The best dietary advice in decades is the idea that a couple of glasses of wine a day protect us all against heart disease. Statistics show that the life expectancy of total abstainers is somewhat less than that of moderate social drinkers.

No one can argue against the very real dangers of excessive alcohol consumption, but sticking to the guidelines of 14 units of alcohol a week for women and 21 units for men appears to pose no risk and seems to convey considerable benefits. One 'official' unit of alcohol is the equivalent of a small glass of wine, a pub measure of spirits or half a pint of normal-strength beer.

Contrary to what most people believe, however, alcohol is a depressant – not a stimulant. Yet it is the way in which alcohol depresses the inhibitory centres of the brain that gives it its relaxing and mood-enhancing properties. That is why these Booze Juices have been included in this book: they are a collection of delicious recipes designed for special, relaxing moments. They also supply a shot of antioxidants to protect you against the damaging effects of alcohol, and give you a glassful of healthy vitamins, minerals and other phytonutrients into the bargain. Can you think of a better way to say 'Cheers'?

a hair of the dog

If you made the great mistake of having a night on the tiles, then this is probably what you need for that infamous morning after. Radishes help cleanse the liver. Carrots provide a massive boost of vitamin A (also good for the liver), and apples are among Nature's great detoxifiers. To make this drink, juice the fruit and vegetables, then stir the vodka into the finished juice.

carrots 6, unpeeled; unless organic, remove top and bottom

radishes 4, with leaves

apples 2, unpeeled, uncored and quartered

vodka 1 shot

vital statistics
Super-rich in **vitamin A**, **beta-carotene** and other **carotenoids**. Rich in **potassium**. Contains **vitamin C**. This Superjuice is not only cleansing and healing to the liver, but the natural soluble fibre **pectin** from apples stimulates the digestive system and helps remove the alcoholic by-products from your body. Vodka, by the way, is one of the purest spirits available, and contains virtually no additives.

virgin fantasy

Here is an anytime cocktail that combines the wonderful
flavours of its ingredients with a modest alcoholic buzz. Add
some black pepper and Worcestershire sauce if you like, and
enjoy, knowing that you're doing your heart and kidneys a
favour at the same time. To make this drink, juice the fresh
ingredients, then stir the vodka into the finished juice.

tomatoes 6 medium, ripe

carrots 2, unpeeled; unless organic, remove top and bottom

celery 1 stick, with leaves

parsley 1 handful, with stems

vodka 2 shots

vital statistics
Super-rich in **vitamin A** and **C**, **carotenoids**
and **lycopene**. Rich in **folic acid** and **potassium**.
Its vitamin A content makes this a good Booze Juice for
skin and eyes, as well as giving a boost to the immune
system. The high content of lycopene also makes this a
heart protector, and the combined effects of celery and
parsley stimulate the activity of the kidneys.

healer colada

If you need an excuse for this delicious drink, then tell your friends it's great for sore throats (as well as a tasty cure for indigestion). Surprisingly, the Healer Colada also guards against the formation of blood clots, so it is protective against both strokes and heart disease. To make it, first juice the pineapple, then stir in the coconut milk and rum.

pineapple 1 medium, unpeeled but remove top
coconut milk 175 ml (6 fl oz)
white rum 2 shots

vital statistics
Rich in **vitamin C**. Not a terrific source of any other nutrients, but the Healer Colada does contain an abundance of a remarkable enzyme called **bromelane**. This constituent speeds up digestion – especially of all types of meat – and it also has the ability to break down any blood clots that might be forming in the circulatory system. Add the modest dose of alcohol and you're really taking care of your heart.

pink punch

This pink delight has universal taste appeal. The subtle blends of sweet flavours from the strawberries and cherries mingle with the tartness of the cranberries and grapefruit to produce an exceptionally clean-tasting, refreshing juice. Although alcohol isn't ideal for anyone with cystitis, if you must booze, then this is the juice to choose. To make this drink, juice the fruit, then stir the vodka into the finished juice.

*pink grapefruit 1, peeled, but leaving pith on
cherries 175 g (6 oz), stoned
cranberries 175 g (6 oz)
strawberries 175 g (6 oz)
vodka 2 shots

*If taking prescribed medicines, consult your doctor before drinking large amounts of grapefruit juice.

vital statistics
Super-rich in **vitamin C**. Rich in **vitamin A**, **B complex** and **folic acid**. Contains **calcium**, **potassium**, **sulphur** and **bioflavonoids**.
The great medicinal benefit of cranberry juice is its protective, curative effect on cystitis – equally effective for men and women. But this Booze Juice is also an immensely powerful immune booster and cancer fighter, thanks to the **phytochemicals** in the berries, cherries and grapefruit.

whisky mcvital

Whether you're going down with a cold or flu, or getting over either, this is the perfect comfort drink. When the Scots invented whisky, they named it *uisge beatha*, Gaelic for 'water of life' – and they weren't wrong. Combined with the ginger, especially as a hot toddy, the warming benefits of Whisky McVital are instantly apparent. But it does you good, too, thanks to the nutritional value of the fruit juices. To make this drink, juice the citrus fruit and grapes, then stir the whisky into the finished juice. Top up with boiling water if making a hot toddy.

oranges 2, peeled, but leaving pith on

lime 1, peeled (unless key lime)

lemon 1, peeled

white grapes 175 g (6 oz)

ginger 15 g (½ oz) fresh root, peeled and sliced

whisky 2 shots, stirred into finished juice

boiling water (optional)

vital statistics
Super-rich in **vitamin C** and **bioflavonoids**. Contains **carotenoids** and **calcium**. As well as the immune-boosting, defensive properties of this very high dose of vitamin C, Whisky McVital also contains **gingerols** from the ginger, which stimulate the circulation and produce a strong expectorant effect which helps if you've got a cough.

kentucky comforter

This southern comforter conjures up images of American colonial verandas, rocking chairs and hot, lazy evenings. It's just the thing as an after-dinner drink to improve the digestion, settle the stomach and ensure a good night's sleep, free from heartburn. Fresh mint is the best of all natural antacids, and its flavour combines perfectly with bourbon. To make this drink, first juice the fresh ingredients, then stir the bourbon into the finished juice. Pour into a large glass filled with plenty of ice. Drink deep, y'all!

apples 6, unpeeled, uncored and quartered

mint 6 leaves

sweet potato 1 medium, cut in strips

bourbon 2 shots

ice cubes 1 handful

vital statistics
Super-rich in **vitamins A** and **C**. Contains **carotenoids**, **potassium** and **phosphorus**. **Pectin** from the apples – a natural form of soluble fibre – aids the digestion. Together with the ellagic acid (also from apples), it improves the body's powers of elimination. Sweet potato adds lots of healthy **beta-carotene** (along with the traditional flavours of the South). The aromatic oils in mint protect against digestive discomfort. They increase the flow of bile to improve fat digestion, and relax the muscles of the stomach and colon.

quick, quick, sloe

If anything is guaranteed to get your feet tapping, it is this Booze Juice. Instant energy, instant sunshine in a glass, instant pleasure... all this and more from this exotic combination of nutrient-rich fruits and the unusual flavour of sloe gin. If you can't make your own sloe gin, don't worry; you'll find it in the shops. This juice is beneficial for the skin, eyes and digestion – and for good measure, it's an immune booster, too. To make it, juice the fruit, then stir the sloe gin into the finished juice.

apricots 6, stoned
oranges 2, peeled, but leaving the pith behind
peaches 2, stoned
mango 1, peeled and stoned
sloe gin 2 shots

vital statistics
Super-rich in **vitamins A** and **C**. Contains **potassium**, **calcium** and **magnesium**. Although Quick, Quick, Sloe contains valuable vitamins, it's really the enzymes and protective chemicals that make this such a good juice. Besides its other benefits, it's helpful for fighting chest infections and is also a good juice for anyone with high blood pressure. As if that weren't enough, sloe gin – traditionally a homemade country liquor that's made using wild fruit from the blackthorn bush – is also a good remedy for diarrhoea.

kummel kalma

Kummel is a clear spirit distilled from grain and flavoured with caraway seeds. It's widely popular in northern Europe as a digestif – especially in Holland, its place of origin. Combined here with the cleansing properties of this vegetable mixture, you have the ideal remedy for bloating, distension, wind and indigestion. To make this drink, first juice the fruit and vegetables, then stir the kummel into the finished juice.

carrots 4, unpeeled; unless organic, remove top and bottom

cabbage 2 leaves

celery 2 sticks, with leaves if possible

apple 1, unpeeled, uncored and quartered

beetroot ½, unpeeled, with leaves

kummel 2 shots

vital statistics
Super-rich in **vitamins A, C, E** and **folic acid** and **potassium**. Contains **calcium**, **magnesium**, **niacin** and **vitamin B$_6$**. This is a good anti-cancer cocktail, thanks to the cabbage and beetroot. It also provides a gentle diuretic effect, thanks to the celery, and the high content of vitamins A and E means that it's good for the circulation and skin, too. The **volatile oils** from the caraway seeds in the kummel are known to act directly on the whole digestive system.

calvados cure-all

A cure-all for colds, flu, headache, backache, toothache, rheumatism, lethargy and listlessness, and the ideal juice for anyone who is just plain sick and tired of being sick and tired. This drink is perfect after a day in the cold (or even a day when you can't be bothered to go out in the cold). The tonic effects of ginger and cloves and all the health benefits of apples and lemons complement the fiery zest of calvados, the traditional apple brandy of Normandy. Stir the calvados into the finished juice, then add enough boiling water to make a hot toddy.

apples 2, unpeeled, uncored and quartered

lemons 2, with peel unless thin-skinned

cloves 2 whole

ginger 25 g (1 oz) fresh root, peeled and sliced

honey 1 dessertspoon

calvados 2 shots

boiling water

vital statistics
Super-rich in **vitamin C** and **bioflavonoids**. Contains **B-complex vitamins**, **folic acid**, **manganese** and **iron**. This Booze Juice is seriously curative. At the first signs of a cold or flu take a large, hot glassful and get an early night. The **gingerols** – volatile oils in ginger – open up the blood vessels and get your circulation whizzing, increasing temperature and sweating. You'll feel great by the morning.

rain forest freezer

I was floating through the Brazilian rain forest in a boat on the Amazon when I had my first taste of Caipirinha – the national cocktail of Brazil. It's traditionally made from a white rum distilled from sugar cane called *cachaça*, chopped limes and lots of ice and sugar. In the overwhelming heat and humidity of the rain forest, it's cool and refreshing and tastes like lemonade. Beware! Its effects creep up on the uninitiated. To make this drink, first juice the whole lime, papaya and pineapple. Put the ice in a large glass. Add the remaining ingredients to the glass, then pour in the finished juice and stir.

lime 1, unpeeled

papaya 1, deseeded, flesh scooped out of skin

pineapple 1 thick slice, unpeeled

ice cubes 1 handful

cachaça (or other white rum), 2 shots

guarana 2 teaspoons of extract

lime 1, unpeeled, cut in small pieces

sugar 2 teaspoons

vital statistics
Super-rich in **vitamin C**. Rich in **vitamin A** and **carotenoids**. Bring a little sunshine into a dull, rainy day with this wonderful cocktail. Naturally, it's also a great drink on a hot summer's afternoon and the slow-release energy from the guarana will help offset the almost irresistible desire to have 'just one more'. The Brazilian rain forest Indians have used the amazing properties of the guarana seed for more than 1,000 years to help them survive the rigours of jungle life.

shakes & smoothies

Shakes and Smoothies may sound like little more than a tasty indulgence, but nothing could be further from the truth. They can provide a meal in a glass, a convalescent's first steps on the road to recovery, a vegetable-hating child's salvation and the busy person's brilliant alternative to instant TV dinners.

The most unlikely but nutritionally excellent ingredients can go into your blender – a far cry from the burger bar's high-fat, low-nutrient milkshakes. Some of these recipes need a blender (if you don't have one, then the hand-held magic wand types work fairly well, even if they take a bit longer). Others require a juicer and a blender. Don't be put off by the need for equipment: these Superjuices are honestly worth the effort and the washing up.

Milk, yogurt and frozen yogurt, soya milk and yogurt, ice cream of all types (including soya), fruits, dried fruits, nuts, seeds, fortifying nutritional ingredients such as wheat germ, lecithin, brewer's yeast, kelp, molasses, even vitamin C... all are included in the following recipes. However, the ingredients can be tailored to your individual needs as well as tastes. Shakes and Smoothies also provide the ideal opportunity to include herbs and spices – especially those that have good effects on the digestive system. Nutmeg, cinnamon, cloves, ginger, mint and chillies are just a few examples. You'll find even more in the recipes themselves. Whether you need to gain or lose weight, Shakes and Smoothies can help, as each glassful provides a super-abundance of nutrients. What's more, this chapter includes recipes suitable for all ages – from toddlers to pensioners.

Of course, the idea of Shakes and Smoothies is nothing new. As devotees of Indian food know, drinks made from yoghurt are a favourite throughout India. They're ideal partners for hot, spicy food since capsaicin, the substance that makes chillies hot, dissolves in fat – not water. These recipes, however, are different from the typical Indian restaurant offerings, since the ingredients they contain are designed – as is everything in this book – specifically with good health in mind.

monkey business

This might sound like a kid's party treat – most children will love it – but it's also a real energy-boosting and nutritious Smoothie. Instantly available calories from the fruit sugar in the apples are mixed with the slower-release calories in the bananas to make this a suitable drink to take before sustained physical activity. As any athlete will tell you, bananas prevent cramp. Make sure you select one of the healthy peanut butters, without added salt. To make this Smoothie, juice the apples, then blend with the bananas and peanut butter.

apples 6, unpeeled, uncored and quartered
bananas 2, peeled
peanut butter 1 tablespoon smooth

vital statistics
Super-rich in **vitamin C** and **potassium**. Contains **vitamin A**. Apples provide large quantities of the soluble fibre **pectin** which, together with the ulcer-fighting benefits of bananas, make this smoothie suitable for all digestive problems. The high content of **ellagic acid** from apples provides valuable cancer protection, and peanut butter supplies valuable **protein**, as well as **iron**, magnesium, vitamin E and folic acid.

jungle jive

A good start to any day is with the wide-awake flavours of mango and passion-fruit. Drink this shake for breakfast, then follow it with a bowl of wholegrain cereal or some wholemeal toast and honey, and you won't be craving sticky buns by the middle of the morning. To make it, first juice the mango and passion fruit, then blend with the milk and yoghurt.

passion fruit 2, seeds scooped out into juicer
mango 1, peeled and stoned
frozen yogurt 140 g (5 oz) live, low-fat
skimmed milk 300 (½ pint)

vital statistics
Super-rich in **calcium**, **potassium** and **flavonoids**. Contains **vitamins A** and **C**. These tropical fruits are laden with protective **antioxidants**. Their high enzyme content is good for digestion; passion fruit in particular is helpful in the relief of gout and arthritis. When combined with almost a day's requirement of calcium, mango and passion fruit make this a fabulous morning mixture.

shakes & smoothies

lime-e shake

A bonanza for blood and bones. Here's another shake with virtually a whole day's calcium needs, as well as the vitamin C quotient you'd expect from citrus fruits. The bonus, however, comes from the wheat germ which simply oozes with B vitamins and vitamin E. Low in calories, high in antioxidants, Lime-E Shake should be the choice for anyone recovering from illness, or under excessive stress. To make it, first juice the oranges and lime, leaving as much pith on as possible, and then blend with the other ingredients.

oranges 2, peeled, but leaving pith on

lime 1, peeled (unless key lime)

banana 1, peeled

skimmed milk 300 ml (½ pint)

yogurt 140 g (5 oz) live, low-fat

wheat germ 2 heaped tablespoons

vital statistics

Super-rich in **vitamin C**, **potassium**, **calcium**. Rich in **B vitamins** and **vitamin E**. Contains **bioflavonoids**, **iron** and **magnesium**. Abundant amounts of vitamin C are essential for healing and low intakes of this nutrient are known to delay wound-healing after surgery. If you've just had an operation, this shake will assist you on the road to a speedy recovery and protect you against infection into the bargain.

paradiso

Just the aroma of mango, pineapple, lime and ginger transports you to paradise. Drinking these juices is a passport to good health and vitality. Whipped into a cooling, frothy shake with live yogurt, this combination is invigorating, restoring and protective. It's wonderful for children (though some prefer it without the ginger) and perfect in the early stages of pregnancy, as ginger helps prevent morning sickness. To make it, first juice the mango, pineapple, ginger and lime, then blend with the yogurt and a handful of ice cubes.

lime 1, peeled (unless key lime)

mango 1, peeled and stoned

pineapple 1, top removed

ginger 25 g (1 oz) fresh root, peeled and sliced

yoghurt 140 g (5 oz) live, low-fat

ice cubes 1 handful

vital statistics
Super-rich in **vitamins A**, **C** and **bioflavonoids**. Rich in **calcium**. Contains some **B vitamins**, **phosphorus**, **copper**, **iron** and **magnesium**. The healing enzyme bromelain in the pineapple, the vitamin A in the mango and vitamin C with **bioflavonoids** in the lime make this one of the most comprehensive protectors around. Add the beneficial bacteria in yogurt and you'll see why Paradiso is one of the healthiest Shakes you can drink.

spice island special

You can almost hear the sound of breakers on the coral reef when you smell this mixture of coconut, cinnamon and cloves. The addition of a shot of Jamaican rum is entirely optional, but totally delicious. This drink is of special value to women – though, of course, men can enjoy it, too. It's the amazing benefits of soya which protect against breast cancer that contribute to its value. To make it, blend all the ingredients with a handful of ice-cubes.

soya milk 300 ml (½ pint)
coconut milk 150 ml (¼ pint)
frozen yogurt 140 g (5 oz) live, low-fat
ground cinnamon ½ teaspoon
ground cloves ¼ teaspoon
ice cubes 1 handful

vital statistics
Contains **protein**, **calcium**, **iron** and some **B vitamins**. This shake is not included for normal nutritional reasons, although the small amounts of iron are better absorbed than those from most non-meat sources. The yogurt provides calcium, while the cinnamon, cloves and beneficial bacteria are all digestive aids. It's really for the enormous cancer-fighting benefits present in soya products that Spice Island Special should be drunk on a regular basis.

spiced silk

The historic use of sesame and cumin goes back to ancient Egypt and China. Cumin is referred to in the Old Testament, and sesame seeds were found in the tomb of Tutankhamun. Both these seeds help to improve the flow of breast milk in nursing mothers, and they are also digestive aids. When combined with the friendly bacteria in yogurt, this makes for a powerfully effective shake. To make it, simply blend the yogurt, tahini and cumin with a handful of ice cubes, then pour into a glass and sprinkle sesame seeds on top.

yogurt 280 g (10 oz) live, low-fat
tahini 1 tablespoon
cumin seeds ½ teaspoon crushed
ice cubes 1 handful
sesame seeds 1 teaspoon

vital statistics

Rich in the **B vitamin niacin**, **folic acid**, **calcium**, **zinc** and **vitamin E**. Contains **protein** and **B vitamins**. Cumin seeds contain volatile oils, especially **pinene** and **terpene**, and it's these that have a direct action on the muscles of the gut. Sesame seeds are an excellent source of the health-giving linoleic acids, and contain lots of protein, calcium and other nutrients.

the guardian

No vampire is going to sink their fangs into your neck after this garlic-laden tipple! But of course, garlic is powerfully antiseptic and wards off bugs as well as vampires. Mixed here with the heart-protective tomatoes and immune-boosting carrots, this Smoothie is the best excuse ever for a circulation-improving tipple. Enjoy it with a friend and a clear conscience. To make it, first juice the vegetables, then blend with crushed ice and vodka and add the lemon chunks.

tomatoes 6 medium

carrots 2, unpeeled; unless organic, remove top and bottom

celery 2 sticks, with leaves

garlic 2 cloves, peeled

ice crushed

vodka 2 shots

lemon 1, with peel, cut in small chunks

vital statistics
Super-rich in **vitamins A, C, folic acid** and **potassium**. Contains some **calcium, phosphorus** and **magnesium**. The Guardian is a powerful immune stimulator, not only due to its high content of vitamins A and C, but also because of the coumarins in celery. These natural chemicals enhance the activity of white cells, an essential part of the body's natural defences. The heart-protecting lycopene from tomatoes combines with the all-round heart and circulatory protection gained from garlic.

shakes & smoothies

green dream

If you're feeling a bit jaded, lacking in energy, and your skin's beginning to look tired, dry and wrinkly, serve up this Smoothie at least a couple of times a week. It lifts the spirits, thanks to the mood-enhancing effect of nutmeg, and the avocado works wonders on the skin. To make Green Dream, put all the ingredients in the blender with a handful of ice-cubes.

avocado 1 large, peeled and stoned

kelp powder 1 dessertspoon

nutmeg a generous grind

skimmed milk 300 ml (½ pint)

yogurt 140 g (5 oz) live, low-fat

ice cubes 1 handful

vital statistics

Super-rich in **calcium**, **vitamins E** and **B₁**. Rich in **folic acid** and **iodine**. Contains **protein** and some **vitamin D**. Iodine is essential for the normal function of the thyroid gland, and few of the patients I see have a sufficient amount of this essential mineral in their diets. Deficiency can lead to chronic fatigue. It's not just the vitamin E in avocados that's good for the skin; they also contain natural chemicals that stimulate the production of collagen, which smoothes out the wrinkles and gives young skin its wonderful bloom.

mock mint choc

You don't have to wait till after eight to enjoy the delicious chocolate-mint flavour of this soya milkshake. You get all the nutritional benefits of carob without the fat and sugar content of chocolate. Masses of protein for long-term staying power, a quick energy boost from the honey and milk sugar in the yogurt, together with the digestive benefits of mint, make this an all-round winner. To create this Shake, put the Brazil nuts in the blender first; when they're finely ground, add the other ingredients.

brazil nuts 5, shelled

mint 6 leaves

soya milk 300 ml (½ pint)

yogurt 140 g (5 oz) live, low-fat

honey 1 dessertspoon

carob powder 2 dessertspoons

vital statistics
Super-rich in **calcium** and **selenium**. Rich in **protein** and **potassium**. Contains **iron**. As well as the amazing protection against breast cancer gained from soya milk, the Brazil nuts provide a whole day's needs of the trace mineral selenium. This much-ignored vital mineral is essential for normal functioning of the heart and for protection against prostate cancer. The average daily consumption in the UK is less than half the required amount.

body builder

The world appears to be full of people trying to lose weight, but for the permanently skinny, life can be equally miserable. They won't go to the gym, the swimming pool or on beach holidays, and usually try stuffing themselves on unhealthy high-fat foods when what they really need is lots of small meals a day, including plenty of high-calorie, low-bulk foods like the ingredients in this super Shake. When I offered a weight-gain recipe in a national newspaper, we had 15,000 requests! To make the Body Builder, first purée the dates in the blender, then add all the other ingredients. Make this Shake in the morning and drink half of it straight away. Keep the rest in the 'fridge and finish it off in the evening.

dates 4 fresh, stoned

banana 1, peeled

molasses 1 dessertspoon

honey 1 dessertspoon

tahini 1 dessertspoon

wheat germ 1 dessertspoon

brewer's yeast 1 dessertspoon

whole milk 425 ml (¾ pint)

yogurt 140 g (5 oz) live, full-fat

vital statistics
Super-rich in **healthy calories**, **calcium** and **potassium**. Contains **iron**, **vitamin E** and some **B vitamins**. Nuts, seeds, and dried fruits are a terrific source of calories with very little bulk. If you're underweight, it's extremely difficult to eat enough starchy foods to provide the surplus calories required. This Shake tastes great, and its added bonus comes from the dates, believed throughout the Middle East to have aphrodisiac properties. You've been warned!

skinny dip

If you need to lose weight, the one thing that doesn't work is going without food, feeling hungry and trying to stick to a very low-calorie diet. Reduce the amount of fat you consume and increase your physical activity: eat two slices of bread and butter a day less and walk 15 minutes a day more and you'll lose a pound a week. This Smoothie is filling, sustaining, nourishing, tasty and low in calories. To make it, simply juice the vegetables, then blend with other ingredients.

tomatoes 6 medium

celery 2 sticks, with leaves

parsley 1 handful, with stems

yogurt 140 g (5 oz) live, very low-fat

cottage cheese 115 g (4 oz) very low-fat

brewer's yeast 2 teaspoons

worcestershire sauce to taste

vital statistics
Super-rich in **vitamin C** and **carotenoids**.
Rich in **calcium**. Contains **B vitamins**, **potassium**
and **protein**. Use Skinny Dip to replace one meal a day.
The recipe will make a thick, creamy Smoothie, but by
adding more cottage cheese and less yogurt, you can make
it thick enough to use as a dip. Eat it with a selection
of crudités, such as celery, carrot, fennel, broccoli,
cauliflower and peppers.

agen provocateur

The best prunes in the world come from the small French town of Agen, where they've been grown for more than 800 years. Look out for *Pruneaux d'Agen* on the package, which means the same as *appellation contrôlée* on a bottle of fine wine. Prunes are famed for their gentle laxative action, but because of their high potassium content, they're good for high blood pressure, too. To make this Smoothie, first juice the apples and pears and purée the prunes in the blender, then add the juice, lecithin and molasses and blend together.

apples 4, unpeeled, uncored and quartered

pears 4, unpeeled

prunes 6, soaked and stoned

lecithin granules 1 dessertspoon

molasses 1 dessertspoon

vital statistics
Super-rich in **vitamin C**. Rich in **potassium**. Contains **vitamin E**. This Smoothie has a wide range of health benefits. It's good for digestion and constipation, and ideal for those suffering from arthritis, rheumatism or gout. The **lecithin** helps improve brain function and memory, and the extra **iron** and potassium from molasses, together with the enormous amount of soluble fibre from the apples and pears, lowers cholesterol, reduces blood pressure and protects the heart.

the natural pharmacy

As you'll have gathered by now, the fruits, vegetables, nuts, seeds and other ingredients used to make Superjuices are not included just because they taste good. Each and every one of them plays a fundamental role in helping to avoid and overcome a variety of illnesses. Even the most commonplace ingredient is a pharmaceutical factory, manufacturing and storing hundreds of different substances known as phyto- ('plant') nutrients. These are not just the essential vitamins miraculously produced in leaves, roots, fruits, nuts and seeds; they also include complex chemical substances with specific health benefits.

For example, both vitamin A and the plant-based beta-carotene have specific cancer-fighting properties. Other carotenoids such as lutein, xeaxanthine and lycopene protect the eyes and heart. Vitamin C is best known for its antioxidant and protective powers, but studies around the world show that where diets are richest in foods containing vitamin C, people suffer less cancer. Not long ago, vitamin E was thought essential only for animal reproductive function; there was no corresponding proof in humans. Today, we know that it is vital in the battle against heart disease. Similarly, deficiencies of folic acid, selenium and soluble fibre were once dismissed as relatively unimportant. It's now known that these easily available nutrients can make the difference between good health or life-threatening disease. As well as the vitamin and mineral content of the nutrients listed in the following tables, you'll find frequent references to other phytochemicals in the Superjuice recipes. These are almost always complex substances now known to have undisputed cancer-fighting benefits. Nutrients in cruciferous vegetables; coloured pigments in berries, cherries and beetroot; limonene in citrus fruits... all these and many more exert unimaginable protective influences on human health. As I have said throughout this book, there is no better source of these phyto-nutrients than homemade, freshly prepared Superjuices. Making the most of them is up to you.

the natural pharmacy

raw ingredients a–z

ingredient	source of:
Alfalfa sprouts	Calcium, silicon, vitamins A, B complex, C, E and K
Apples	Carotenes, ellagic acid, pectin, potassium, vitamin C
Apricots	Beta-carotene, iron, potassium, soluble fibre
Artichokes, Jerusalem	Inulin, iron, phosphorus
Asparagus	Asparagine, folic acid, potassium, phosphorus, riboflavin, vitamin C
Banana	Energy, fibre, folic acid, magnesium, potassium, vitamin A
Basil	Volatile oils: linalol, limonene, estragole
Beetroot	Beta-carotene, calcium, folic acid, iron, potassium, vitamins B_6 and C
Blackcurrants	Anti-inflammatory and cancer-fighting phytochemicals, carotenoids, vitamin C
Blueberries	Anti-bacterial and cancer-fighting phytochemicals, carotenoids, vitamin C
Brazil nuts	Protein, selenium, vitamins B and E
Brewer's yeast	B vitamins, biotin, folic acid, iron, magnesium, zinc
Broccoli	Cancer-fighting phytochemicals, folic acid, iron, potassium, riboflavin, vitamins A and C
Cabbage family	Cancer-fighting phytochemicals, folic acid, potassium, vitamins A, C and E
Carrots	Carotenoids, folic acid, magnesium, potassium, vitamin A
Celery	Coumarins, potassium, vitamin C
Chard (Swiss)	Calcium, cancer-fighting phytochemicals, carotenes, iron, phosphorus, vitamins A and C
Cherries	Cancer-fighting phytochemicals, flavonoids, magnesium, potassium, vitamin C
Chicory	Bitter, liver-stimulating terpenoids, folic acid, iron, potassium, vitamin A (if unblanched)
Chives	Beta-carotene, cancer-fighting phytochemicals, vitamin C
Cinnamon	Coumarins, tannins and volatile oils with mild, sedative/analgesic blood pressure-lowering effects
Cloves	Volatile oil (especially eugenol) with anti-nausea, antiseptic, anti-bacterial and analgesic properties
Coconut milk	Calcium, magnesium, potassium, small quantities of B vitamins
Coriander	Coumarins, flavonoids, linalol
Cottage cheese	B vitamins, calcium, folic acid, magnesium, protein, vitamin A
Cranberries	Cancer-fighting phytochemicals, specific urinary anti-bacterials, vitamin C
Cucumber	Folic acid, potassium, silica, small amounts of beta-carotene in the skin
Cumin seeds	Flavonoids which relieve intestinal wind and spasm, volatile oils
Dandelion	Beta-carotene, diuretic and liver-stimulating phytochemicals, iron, other carotenoids
Dates	Fibre, folic acid, fruit sugar, iron, potassium
Fennel	volatile oils: fenchone, anethole and anisic acid, all liver and digestive stimulants
Figs	Beta-carotene, cancer-fighting phytochemicals, fibre, ficin (a digestive aid) iron, potassium
Garlic	Anti-bacterial and antifungal sulphur compounds, cancer- and heart disease-fighting phytochemicals

ingredient	source of:
Ginger	Circulatory-stimulating zingiberene and gingerols
Grapes	Natural sugars, powerful antioxidant flavonoids, vitamin C
Grapefruit	Beta-carotene, bioflavonoids (especially naringin, which thins the blood and lowers cholesterol), vitamin C
Horseradish	Natural antibiotics, protective phytochemicals, vitamin C
Jalapeño pepper	Carotenoids, capsaicin (a circulatory stimulant), flavonoids
Kale	Beta-carotene, calcium, cancer-fighting phytochemicals, folic acid, iron, phosphorus, sulphur, vitamin C
Kiwi fruit	Beta-carotene, bioflavonoids, fibre, potassium, vitamin C
Kohlrabi	Cancer-fighting phytochemicals, folic acid, potassium, vitamin C
Lamb's lettuce	Folic acid, iron, potassium, vitamins A, C and B_6, zinc. Also contains calming phytochemicals
Lecithin	Phospholipids extracted from soya beans: heart protective and beneficial to nerves
Leeks	Anti-arthritic, anti-inflammatory substances, cancer-fighting phytochemicals, folic acid, potassium, diuretic substances, vitamins A and C
Lemon	Bioflavonoids, limonene, potassium, vitamin C
Lettuce	Calcium, folic acid, phosphorus, potassium, sleep-inducing phytochemicals, vitamins A and C
Lime	Bioflavonoids, limonene, potassium, vitamin C
Mango	Beta-carotene, flavonoids, potassium, other antioxidants, vitamin C
Mangosteen	Digestive-friendly mucilage, potassium, vitamin C
Melon	Folic acid, potassium, small amounts of B vitamins, vitamins A and C
Milk	Calcium, protein, riboflavin, zinc
Mint	Antispasmodic volatile oils, flavonoids, menthol
Mixed salad leaves	Calcium, folic acid, phosphorus, potassium, sleep-inducing phytochemicals (the darkest leaves contain the most nutrients), vitamins A and C
Molasses	Calcium, iron, magnesium, phosphorus
Mooli	Iron, magnesium, phytochemicals that stimulate the gall bladder and heal mucous membranes, potassium, vitamin C
Nutmeg	Myristicin (mood enhancing and hallucinogenic in excess); phytochemicals that aid sleep and digestion
Oranges and citrus (including mandarins, satsumas and tangerines)	Bioflavonoids, calcium, folic acid, iron, limonene, potassium, thiamine, vitamins B_6 and C
Pak choi	Beta-carotene, B vitamins, cancer-fighting phytochemicals, folic acid, vitamin C
Parsley	Calcium, iron, potassium, vitamins A and C
Parsnip	B vitamins, folic acid, inulin, potassium, vitamin E
Passion-fruit	Beta-carotene, phytochemicals which are antiseptic, sedative and mildly laxative, vitamin C
Pawpaw	Beta-carotene, flavonoids, magnesium, papain (a digestive enzyme), vitamin C
Peaches	Beta-carotene, flavonoids, potassium, vitamin C
Peanuts	B vitamins, folic acid, protein, iron, zinc
Pears	Soluble fibre, vitamin C
Peppers	Beta-carotene, folic acid, potassium, phytochemicals that prevent blood clots, strokes and heart disease, vitamin C

ingredient	source of:
Pineapple	Enzymes (especially bromelain, helpful for angina, arthritis and physical injury), vitamin C
Plums	Beta-carotene, malic acid (an effective aid to digestion), vitamins C and E
Pomegranate	Beta-carotene, enzymes with anti-diarrhoeal properties, heart-protective phytochemicals, vitamin E
Prunes	Beta-carotene, fibre, iron, niacin, potassium, vitamin B_6
Pumpkin	Folic acid, potassium, small amounts of B vitamins, vitamins A and C
Purslane	Essential fatty acids, cleansing bitter alkaloids, folic acid, vitamins C and E
Radishes	Iron, magnesium, phytochemicals that stimulate gall bladder and heal mucous membranes, potassium, vitamin C
Rosemary	Flavonoids, volatile oils (borneol, camphor and limonene)
Sage	Phenolic acids, phyto-oestrogens, thujone: an antiseptic
Sauerkraut	Calcium, cancer-fighting phytochemicals, gut-protective lactic acid, potassium, vitamin C
Seaweed	Beta-carotene, calcium, iodine, iron, protein, magnesium, potassium, soluble fibre, vitamin B_{12}, zinc
Sesame seeds	B vitamins, calcium, folic acid, magnesium, niacin, protein, vitamin E
Sorrel	Carotenoids, iron, protective phytochemicals, vitamin C
Soya milk	Calcium, phytoestrogens especially genistein (a powerful breast, ovarian and prostate cancer-fighter), protein. If fortified, also vitamin D
Spinach	Beta-carotene, cancer-fighting phytochemicals, chlorophyll, folic acid, iron, lutein, xeaxanthine
Spring greens	Beta-carotene, cancer-fighting phytochemicals, carotenoids, iron, vitamin C
Spring onion	Cancer-fighting phytochemicals, diuretic, anti-arthritic and anti-inflammatory substances, folic acid, potassium, vitamins A and C
Stinging nettle	Beta-carotene, calcium, iron, vitamin C
Strawberries	Anti-arthritic phytochemicals, beta-carotene, vitamins C and E
Sweet potato	Beta-carotene and other carotenoids, cancer-fighting phytochemicals, protein, vitamins C and E
Tahini	B vitamins, calcium, folic acid, magnesium, niacin, protein, vitamin E
Thyme	Flavonoids, volatile oils (antiseptic thymol and carvol)
Tomatoes	Beta-carotene, lycopene, potassium, vitamins C and E
Watercress	Anti-bacterial mustard oils, beta-carotene, iron, phenethyl isothiocyanate (specific lung cancer fighter for smokers), vitamins C and E
Watermelon	Folic acid, potassium, small amounts of B vitamins, vitamins A and C
Wheat germ	B vitamins, folic acid, iron, magnesium, potassium, vitamin E
Yogurt: milk	Beneficial bacteria, calcium, protein, riboflavin, zinc
Yogurt: soya	calcium, phytoestrogens, especially genistein (a powerful breast, ovarian and prostate cancer fighter). If fortified, also contains vitamin D

vitamins and minerals a–z

There's no doubt that vitamin and mineral supplements have a valuable role to play both in the prevention and treatment of a wide variety of health problems. However, what you get from a pill is something that has been artificially manufactured – often with a higher potency than is necessary for good health. In addition, the latest supplements are only what the scientists currently know about, and history warns us that there must be many nutrients waiting to be discovered. There is also a growing amount of evidence that naturally derived vitamins are more effective than those which are synthetically manufactured, since they are purer in origin and, in many cases, more easily absorbed by the body. Based on that information, then, the safest course of action to take for a healthy lifestyle is to ensure that you get an adequate supply of all essential nutrients from your food. The best way to do that, of course, is through the regular consumption of your own freshly produced Superjuices.

The following tables show which vitamins and minerals you need for good health, what they do and the food sources from which they can be obtained.

vitamins	essential for:	best food sources:
A	Growth, skin, colour and night vision, immunity	Butter, cheese, chicken liver, cod liver oil, eggs, herring, lambs' liver, mackerel, salmon
B_1 (Thiamine)	Conversion of starchy foods into energy	Brewer's yeast (dried), peanuts, peanut butter, pork and pork products, sunflower seeds, vegetarian burger mixes, wheat germ, yeast extracts
B_2 (Riboflavin)	Converting fats and proteins into energy, also for mucous membranes and skin	Brewer's yeast, cheese, eggs, green leafy vegetables, liver, meat, soya products, wheat germ, yeast extracts, yogurt
B_3 (Niacin)	Brain and nerve function, healthy skin, tongue and digestive organs	Brewer's yeast (dried), cheese, dried fruits, eggs, nuts, oily fish, pigs' liver, poultry, wholegrain cereals, yeast extracts
B_6 (Pyridoxine)	Protein conversion, protection against heart disease, regulation of menstrual cycle, growth, nervous and immune systems	Bananas, beef, brewer's yeast, cod, herring, lentils, poultry, salmon, walnuts, wheat germ
B_{12}	Metabolism, nervous system, prevention of pernicious anaemia, proper formation of blood cells. With B_6, controls levels of homocysteine, which may cause heart disease	Beef, cheese, eggs, lamb, liver, oily fish, pork, seaweed

vitamins	essential for:	best food sources:
Beta-carotene	Essential in its own right for protection against heart disease, cancer and as an immune-booster. Not a vitamin in its own right, but listed here as it is also converted by the body into vitamin A (see previous page)	Apricots, chard, dark green and red-leaf lettuce, dark leafy greens, mangoes, old carrots, pumpkin, red and yellow peppers, spinach, squashes, sweet potatoes, tomatoes, watercress, yellow melons
C	Natural immunity, wound healing, iron absorption, extremely powerful antioxidant that protects against heart disease, circulatory problems and cancers	All citrus fruits, all green vegetables, berries, currants, lettuces, peppers, potatoes, tomatoes, tropical fruits (guavas, mangoes, kiwi fruits and pineapple)
D	Bone formation, protection from osteoporosis and rickets	Canned sardines, cod liver oil, eggs, fresh tuna, herring, kipper, mackerel, salmon, trout
E	Antioxidant protection of the heart and blood vessels, skin, immune-boosting and cancer-fighting	Avocado, broccoli, nuts and seeds, peanut butter, safflower/ sunflower/olive and other seed oils, spinach, sweet potatoes, watercress, wheat germ
Folic acid	Blood cells, prevention of birth defects, protects against anaemia	Brewer's yeast (dried), citrus fruits, eggs, dried fruits, fresh nuts, green leafy vegetables, liver, oats, pulses, soya flour, wheat germ
Calcium	Bone formation and prevention of osteoporosis, proper functioning of heart muscles and nerves	Brazil nuts, cheese, chickpeas, dried seaweeds, figs, greens, milk, shellfish, tinned sardines, tofu, whitebait, yogurt
Iodine	Normal functioning of the thyroid gland	Cod, cockles, haddock (fresh or smoked), milk, mussels, seaweed, smoked mackerel, whelks
Iron	Red blood cells	Liver, kidney, dried apricots, wholemeal bread, spinach, raisins, prunes, dates, lentils, sesame and pumpkin seeds, legumes, nuts, dark-green leafy vegetables, beef and other meats
Magnesium	Energy-producing processes, the functions of vitamins B_1 and B_6, growth and repair	Almonds, Brazil nuts, brown rice, cashews, peas, pine nuts, sunflower and sesame seeds, soya-based protein, soya beans
Potassium	Normal cell function, nerves, control of blood pressure	Bananas, cheese, dried fruits, eggs, molasses, nuts, fresh fruit, fruit juices, raw vegetables, tea, wholemeal bread
Selenium	Powerful antioxidant: protects against heart disease, prostate cancer and lung cancer	Brazil nuts, dried mushrooms, lambs' kidneys and liver, lentils, sardines, sunflower seeds, tuna, walnuts, white fish, wholemeal bread
Zinc	Growth, hormone function, male fertility, liver function, immunity, taste	Cheese, dried seaweed, eggs, liver, oysters, pumpkin/sesame/ sunflower seeds, pine nuts, shellfish, wholemeal bread

chemical robbery

Many doctors are unaware of the damaging effects some medicines have on nutritional well-being. The depletion of nutrients that results from long-term use of these 'chemical robbers' actually hinders the healing process. Chronic Fatigue Syndrome is a case in point: commonly caused by a zinc deficiency, it can also be a symptom of depression. Anti-depressants will, over time, interfere with zinc absorption – making you even more zinc-deficient and more exhausted and depressed. The following is a list of common drug categories and their long-term effects on nutritional needs. When taking any for an extended period, give your body a boost with the relevant Superjuices in order to counteract or at least balance their effects.

drug category	effect
Antacids	Increase the need for vitamins A, B complex, calcium, magnesium, iron and phosphorus
Antibiotics	Increase the need for B-complex vitamins because they destroy natural bacteria in the gut. Always eat live yogurt every day when taking antibiotics
Anti-coagulants	Including warfarin; aspirin and all their relatives affect vitamin K
Anti-convulsants	Interfere with the body's absorption of vitamins B_6, D and K as well as folic acid. These drugs are normally taken for extended periods of time as in the treatment of epilepsy. Phenytoin (also used to treat irregular heartbeats) interferes with the absorption of calcium
Anti-inflammatory drugs	Sulfasalazine, which is prescribed for inflammatory bowel disease, causes a loss of folic acid. Rather than taking a supplement, it's much better to get your folic acid from a varied diet and fresh juices
Anti-malarial drugs	Can also act against folic acid, and long-term use may cause problems, such as anaemia and vision and hearing disturbances
Anti-ulcer drugs	Reduce the stomach's production of acid and can cause poor absorption of vitamin B_{12}
Cholesterol-lowering drugs	Increase the need for iron, beta-carotene, vitamins A, D, K and folic acid
Diuretics	Many of these drugs deprive the body of B-complex vitamins, potassium, magnesium and zinc
Drugs for high blood pressure	Hydralazine lowers the level of vitamin B_6 in the body
Laxatives	Laxatives cause a considerable loss of vitamins and minerals, especially calcium, phosphorous and vitamin D. This vitamin can be severely affected by long-term use, and its depletion puts women at a greater risk of osteoporosis, since vitamin D is essential for the efficient absorption of calcium
Oral contraceptives	The Pill is a major factor in nutritional status. It adversely affects folic acid, vitamins C and E and B-complex vitamins
Sleeping pills and anti-depressants	Barbiturate-type sleeping pills affect the uptake of vitamin D. Anti-depressants interfere with the chemical process of B_2 absorption as well as with the absorption of the minerals zinc and magnesium
Tranquillizers	Stelazine is detrimental to vitamin B_{12} absorption

drink yourself better

condition	superjuice	effect	dose
Acne	Instant Energizer, p14	Skin-healing and cleansing	4 glasses a week
AMD	Eye Brite, p110	Highly protective carotenoids	2 glasses a week
Anaemia	Super Stinger, p83	Rich in iron and vitamin C	1 glass daily for 2 weeks, then 1 a week
Anxiety	Mediterranean Muscle, p25 Mock Mint Choc, p137	Soothing to the nerves	As required
Arthritis	Ginger Spice, p38 Wake-up Whammy, p94	Anti-inflammatory, pain relieving and energizing	At least 4 glasses a week
Back pain	Papaya Punch, p57 Bunnies Bonanza, p78	Anti-inflammatory, diuretic, analgesic	1 glass daily, alternate between recipes
Blood sugar problems	Savoir Vivre, p100	Instant and slow-release energy to balance sugar levels	1 glass daily
Boils	Primary Pepper Juice, p18	Boosts resistance and detoxifying	1 glass daily if boils present, twice weekly as preventative
Bronchitis	Doctor Garlic, p111	Antibacterial, immune boosting and expectorant	2 glasses daily during infection
Bruising	Oriental Magic, p68	Bromelain reduces bruising	1 glass daily as required
Catarrh	Horse Power, p21	Decongestant, mucous membrane protector	1 glass daily when needed, 2 glasses a week as preventative
Chilblains	Soy Salsa, p106	Stimulates circulation, dilates peripheral blood vessels	2–3 glasses a week during winter
Cholesterol	The Guardian, p135 Dracula's Delight p102	Reduces cholesterol, protects against clotting and a little alcohol stimulates the circulation	At least 3 glasses a week of Dracula; not more than 2 with vodka
Chronic fatigue	Body Builder, p138 Apple and Watercress Energizer, p46	Instant and slow-release energy boosts vitality	1 glass of either recipe daily
Circulation problems	Hot and Juicy, p72	Dilates blood vessels, lowers cholesterol, stimulates circulation	1 glass on alternate days
Colds	C-plus, p82	Provides a huge dose of immune boosting vitamin C, bioflavonoids and echinacea	2 glasses a day throughout cold, and for 2 days afterwards
Constipation	Prune-light Express, p37	Provides masses of gently laxative soluble fibre	1 glass at bedtime
Cough	Doctor Garlic, p111	Antibacterial and expectorant, immune-boosting	1 glass daily until better
Cramp	Buzz Juice, p91 Welsh Ginger, p87	Circulatory stimulant in ginger and extra potassium from banana are both cramp-preventative	1 glass of either recipe in the evening for night cramp, or before sport (if cramp is exercise induced)

condition	superjuice	effect	dose
Cystitis	Pink Punch, p117	Antibacterial, specifically protects (without vodka) against bugs that cause cystitis	1 glass daily during infection, at least 3 glasses a week for prevention
Depression	Skinny Dip, p139 Scarborough Fair, p56	Provides lots of B vitamins and mentally-reviving aromatic oils	1 glass of either, daily
Dermatitis	Spring Clean Tonic, p62	Provides masses of vitamins A and C to stimulate skinhealing	3 glasses a week
Diarrhoea	Sweet Surrender, p71	Fluid replacement. Also harbours natural beneficial bacteria and anti-diarrhoeal properties	1 or 2 glasses daily as required
Diverticulitis	Long-life Lemonade, p98	Provides soluble fibre, healing vitamin A and lots of probiotic bacteria for healthy bowel function	1 glass every other day during acute episodes, twice a week for prevention
Eczema	Passionate Pumpkin, p74	Provides huge amount of skin-healing vitamins A and E	1 glass daily until clear
Fever	Paradiso, p131	Provides anti-inflammatory enzymes, anti-infective essential oils and lots of vitamin C	2 glasses a day until temperature falls
Fibrositis	Dandelion Delight, p31	Strongly diuretic. Eliminates pain-causing uric acid	2–3 glasses a week
Flatulence	The Florentine, p42	Provides soluble fibre for bowel function and anti-flatulence essential oils from fennel	Half a glass after meals
Fluid retention	Dandelion Delight, p31 Radish Revolution, p39	Both juices are strongly diuretic and rich in potassium for a balance of minerals	1 glass of either daily, when necessary
Fractures	Green Dream, p136	Provides lots of calcium and other minerals to speed bone healing	1 glass daily
Gallstones	Octet con Spirito, p63 Radish Revolution, p39	High in fibre to improve digestion. Garlic and radishes specifically stimulate gall bladder and liver function	1 glass of either daily
Gastritis	Lemon Express, p36	Antiseptic, antioxidant and soothing to the stomach lining. For improved benefits, add 1 dessertspoon honey.	2 glasses a day
Gingivitis	Good Mouthkeeping, p103	Antiseptic, antifungal and healing to the gums and mucous membranes of the mouth	1 glass daily, as long as necessary
Gout	Cucumber Soother, p99	Provides soothing enzymes, lots of vitamin A, anti-inflammatory and specific uric acid-reducing properties	1 glass daily during attacks, 2 glasses a week for prevention
Hair problems	Monkey Business, p128 Stir-fry Starter, p84	Contains minerals essential for good hair growth, including iodine, lots of vitamins C and E, and iron	Alternate these juices daily
Halitosis	Oriental Magic, p68	Antibacterial. Also provides healing enzymes and breath-freshening essential oils	1 glass daily, as required
Hay fever	Blue Passion, p51	Provides masses of vitamin C and especially protective bioflavonoids. For extra protection, add a dessertspoon of locally produced honey	1 glass daily
Headache	Femme Fatale, p73	Provides essential fatty acids, vitamins C and E. Stimulates circulation and reduces frequency	1 glass daily until headaches recede, then twice a week

condition	superjuice	effect	dose
Heart disease	Doctor Garlic, p111 Wake-up Whammy, p94	Provides heart-protective lycopenes and beta-carotenes. Also reduces risk of clots, and is a diuretic and a circulatory stimulant	A glass daily
Heartburn	Lime-E Shake, p130	Is soothing, nourishing and provides gut-beneficial bacteria	1 glass as required
Hepatitis	Cherry Ripe, p70 Pro-Bonus 2, p105	Strawberries and cherries are effective liver cleansers. Pro-bonus 2 overflows with liver-nourishing nutrients and phytochemicals	2 glasses of each weekly
Herpes	Rainbow Cocktail, p35	Provides antiviral vitamin C and bioflavonoids	1 glass daily during attacks, 2 glasses weekly for protection
Hypertension	Doctor Garlic, p111 High Flyer, p15	Provides artery-protective phytochemicals and specific blood pressure-lowering properties	1 glass of either daily
Impotence	Spiced Silk, p134	Rich in vitamin E, zinc and selenium for improved function	2 or 3 glasses a week
Indigestion	Lime-E Shake, p130	Soothing, nourishing and provides gut-beneficial bacteria	1 glass as required
Infections	Pro-bonus 1, p104 Back to School, p109	Provide an enormous boost to the natural immune system. Both juices are rich in natural anti-bacterials	1 glass of either daily during illness. At least 2 glasses a week for protection
Infertility	Femme Fatale, p73 Passionate Pumpkin, p74	Provides essential vitamin E, beta-carotenes and minerals for optimum fertility	1 glass of either daily
Influenza	Tropical Revitalizer, p49	Provides soothing enzymes for aches and pains, masses of vitamin C, beta-carotene for resistance and bioflavonoids for protection	1 or 2 glasses daily until you recover
Insomnia	Life Saver, p88	Provides natural sleep-inducing substances in lettuce, together with vitamin C and aromatic oils	1 glass before bed
Joint Pain	Ginger Spice, p38 Wake-up Whammy, p94	Anti-inflammatory, pain relieving and energizing	At least 4 glasses a week
Kidney problems	Waterfall, p29 Pink Punch p117 (without vodka)	Diuretic and antiseptic	1 glass of either daily
Laryngitis	Welsh Ginger, p87 Scarborough Fair, p56	Provides volatile oils which are soothing and antiseptic, as well as the specific voice benefits of leeks	1 glass of either daily, until better. Professional vocalists should drink Welsh Ginger twice a week for protection
Menstrual problems	Femme Fatale, p73 Spice Island Special, p133	Essential fatty acids in purslane, lots of vitamin E, and phytoestrogens in soya milk all help regulate the cycle	1 glass of either daily
Motion and early morning sickness	Ginger Spice, p38 Ginger Up Juice, p69	Volatile oils in ginger prevent sickness	1 glass of either before travelling or as required
Mouth ulcers	Melon and Mango Tango, p22 Good Mouthkeeping, p103	Rich in healing beta-carotenes, natural anti-bacterials and enzymes	1 glass as required. Take regularly for prevention

condition	superjuice	effect	dose
Obesity	Skinny Dip, p139 Agen Provocateur, p141	Full of nutrients, low in calories	1 glass as a replacement for one meal daily
Osteoporosis	Mock Mint Choc, p137 Soy Salsa, p106 Stir-fry Starter, p84	All contain calcium and other trace minerals, selenium, zinc and iron	1 glass of each daily, in rotation
PMS	Spice Island Special, p133 Mountain Rescue, p77	Provides phytoestrogens and essential oils, together with extra iron and enzymes. Also diuretic, so reduces bloating	Alternate 1 glass of each for 7 days before and during the first 2 days of each period
Prostate problems	Watermelon Man, p34	Protective phytochemicals and masses of beta-carotene are prostate protectors. Drink with a handful of pumpkin seeds	1 glass daily until symptoms improve, then 3 times a week
Psoriasis	Passionate Pumpkin, p74	Provides huge amounts of skin-healing vitamins A and E	1 glass daily
Raynaud's Syndrome (constricted circulation in the extremities)	Peppery Pick-up, p89 Calvados Cure-all, p123	Enormous quantities of beta-carotene improve the quality of blood vessels, while the ginger and alcohol in the Cure All dilate blood vessels and stimulate circulation	Alternate 1 glass of either daily during cold weather
Restless legs	Red-eye Special, p16	Provides iron, diuretics and carotenoids to calm this distressing problem	1 glass during the evening as required
Rheumatism	Ginger Spice, p38 Wake-up Whammy, p94	Anti-inflammatory, pain-relieving and energising	At least 4 glasses a week
Seasonal Affective Disorder (SAD)	Women's Wonder, p32 Pepper Purifier, p33	Provides B vitamins, vitamin A and iron. Both these juices provide essential nutrients that also help this condition	Alternate 1 glass of either, daily, during the winter
Shingles	Rainbow Cocktail, p35 Welsh Ginger, p87	Super-rich in antiviral vitamin C and bioflavonoids. Leeks and ginger can be helpful for residual pain	1 glass of either daily, as necessary
Sinusitis	Horse Power p21	Decongestant and mucous membrane protective	1 glass daily when needed, 2 glasses a week as a preventative
Sore throat	Welsh Ginger p87 Scarborough Fair, p56	Provides volatile oils that are soothing and antiseptic; also vocal benefits of leeks	1 glass of either daily. Vocalists should drink Welsh Ginger twice a week for protection
Stomach ulcers	Tutti-frutti, p58	Provides healing bioflavonoids, vitamin C and enzymes. Will be enhanced by adding 1 dessertspoon of honey	1 glass daily
Thyroid problems	Stir-fry Starter, p84	Specially rich in iodine, other trace minerals and vitamin A	2 glasses a week
Tonsillitis	Tropical Revitalizer, p49	Full of protective anti-bacterial nutrients and especially throat-soothing enzymes	3 or 4 small glasses daily
Varicose veins	Quick, Quick, Sloe, p121 Pumping Iron, p23	Quick, Quick, Sloe provides enormous amounts of beta-carotene combined with sloe gin as an occasional circulatory tonic. Pumping Iron provides regular ongoing vascular support	Quick Quick Sloe: no more than twice a week. Pumping Iron: daily

superjuice detox

Sometimes, drastic measures are called for: when you feel stodgy, bloated and run down, you need a short, sharp detox to give your body a rest, recharge the batteries and give the little grey cells a boost. During these four days, you will feel hungry and may get headaches. Don't cheat: avoid painkillers and drink lots of water or herbal teas, but no coffee. Your reward will be a rested liver and digestive system, clear skin, bright eyes and a huge rise in energy levels. By the end of day four you will look and feel great!

If you have diabetes or any serious illness, speak with your healthcare professional before drastically changing your diet.

day one

first thing Large glass of hot water and the juice of a lemon
breakfast Pro-bonus 1 (page 104). One orange, one banana, one kiwi fruit. Herb tea with honey
lunch Pro-bonus 2 (page 105). A salad of tomato, raw broccoli florets, yellow pepper, grated raw beetroot, carrots, radishes and lots of fresh parsley. Drizzle with walnut oil and lime juice
evening meal Peak Performer (page 17). Large mixed salad: red lettuce, watercress, spring onions, garlic, grated raw celeriac and turnip, a sprinkle of toasted pine nuts and finely chopped sage and mint leaves. Add extra-virgin olive oil and lemon juice as a dressing

day two

first thing Large glass of hot water and the juice of a lemon
breakfast Paradiso (see page 131). Herb tea and honey
mid-morning Bunnies' Bonanza (see page 78). Four prunes, four dried apricots and a handful of walnuts and almonds
lunch Long-life Lemonade (see page 98), but omitting the sauerkraut. A large salad of green leaves with radishes, celery, celery leaves, chicory, a sprinkle of sunflower and pumpkin seeds, lemon juice and walnut oil. Herb tea with honey
mid-afternoon Lemon Express (see page 36)

evening meal Spring Clean Tonic (see page 62). A red pepper deseeded and cut in quarters and a large courgette sliced in four, lengthways, drizzle with olive oil and black pepper and cooked on a hot griddle pan or BBQ. Herb tea with honey or weak Indian tea
during the evening One mango, a pear and a pomegranate or two passion fruits

day three

first thing Large glass of hot water and the juice of a lemon
breakfast Blue Passion (see page 51). A carton of live yogurt mixed with a tablespoon of unsweetened muesli. Herb tea with honey
mid-morning Minty Morning (see page 28)
lunch Life Saver (see page 88) A small bowl of raisins, sultanas, Brazil nuts and almonds. Herb tea and honey
mid-afternoon Power Pack (see page 48)
evening meal Waterfall (see page 29). A bowl of pasta with chopped garlic, olive oil and fresh, chopped tomatoes. Half a diced cucumber mixed with low-fat live yogurt and chopped dill or fennel layers. Herb tea with honey

day four

first thing Large glass of hot water and the juice of a lemon
breakfast On Your Mark (see page 92). One poached egg on a whole-grain rice cake, with pepper but NO salt
mid-morning Good Mouthkeeping (see page 103). Six Brazil nuts
lunch Lime-E Shake (see page 130). Steamed spinach topped with finely chopped hazelnuts, a sprinkle of nutmeg and a drizzle of walnut oil; a bowl of mixed berries
mid-afternoon Beet Treat (see page 61)
evening meal Vegetable stir-fry: pea pods, Chinese cabbage, Pak Choi, peas, bean sprouts, leeks and mushrooms. Cook all vegetables except the mushrooms in boiling water for five minutes, then drain. Heat a mix of sesame and peanut oils in a wok, stir in soy sauce, spring onions and garlic, then add the blanched vegetables. Add the mushrooms after two minutes. A papaya. Herb tea with honey

Treat your system gently on Day Five, and don't rush back to normal eating. Avoid red meat, and start with plainly cooked chicken or fish, some wholegrain starchy foods, plenty of fruit, salads and vegetables.

glossary

Age-related Macular Degeneration (AMD) Disease of the retina which results in gradual vision loss, particularly of the ability to focus on or recognize fine detail. The macula lutea is the part of the retina that controls visual acuity.

Anthocyanidins/Anthocyanin Any of the soluble pigments that produce blue to red colouring in flowers and plants.

Antibiotic A substance produced by a micro-organism that is able to inhibit or kill another micro-organism.

Antioxidant A substance that inhibits oxidation. In the body, antioxidants are thought to prevent the destruction of vitamin C, slow the destruction of body cells and strengthen the immune system.

Beta-carotene A powerful antioxidant which the body transforms into vitamin A.

Betanin Substance that produces the red colouring in beetroot

Bile The yellowish-green fluid secreted by the liver that aids digestion and the absorption of fats.

Bioflavonoid Also known as vitamin P, a biologically active flavonoid.

Bromelain An enzyme obtained from pineapple juice.

Capsaicin A colourless irritant found in various capsicums, or peppers.

Carotene Any one of the orange and red pigments that occur in carrots and other plants as well as in egg yolks and butter which is converted into vitamin A.

Carotenoid Any one of the various (usually) yellow to red pigments found widely in plants and animals.

Chlorophyll The green colouring matter in plants.

Chronic Fatigue Syndrome Chronic lethargy or exhaustion that is usually lifestyle related.

Collagen The most abundant protein in the human body and a major structural component of many of its parts, including skin and tendons.

Coumarin A white lactone that beneficially affects blood flow.

Cystitis Inflammation of the bladder.

Diuretic Any substance that increases the production of urine by the kidneys.

Echinacea Native American herb that is beneficial to the immune system. Its anti-microbial properties make it effective in the prevention of colds and flu.

Ellagic acid A natural chemical substance found in some tannins.

Enzyme A chemical substance produced by living cells.

Expectorant Any substance that promotes discharge of mucus from the respiratory tract.

Fatty acid Any of the numerous beneficial fats that occur naturally in fats, waxes and essential oils and are, among other things, good for the heart.

Fenchone A phytochemical in fennel that stimulates the liver.

Flavone A beneficial phytochemical found in leaves, stems and seed capsules of some plants.

Flavonoid A beneficial phytochemical that tends to occur in plants which are high in vitamin C.

Folic acid A vitamin of the B complex used to treat nutritional anaemias.

Free radical Naturally occurring oxygen molecules that damage the body and are thought to play a significant role in the aging process.

Gingerol Volatile oil present in ginger which stimulates circulation.

Gout Metabolic disease marked by painful inflammation of the joints and an excess amount of uric acid in the blood.

Indole A volatile oil of the same family as gingerol (see above).

Inulin A tasteless white substance found mainly in the roots and rhizomes of some plants.

Lactone A beneficial volatile oil.

Lecithin A complex fat found in egg yolks and Brazil nuts. Lecithin contains choline, a substance the body converts into acetylcholine, which is essential for the smooth flow of nerve impulses.

Limonene A substance that occurs in the essential oils of many citrus fruits.

Linoleic acid A liquid unsaturated fatty acid found in oils that is thought to be essential for nutrition.

Lutein A beneficial orange pigment occurring in plants.

Lycopene A carotenoid pigment that forms the colouring matter in tomatoes.

Myalgic Encephalomylitis (ME) A condition involving tiredness, muscle pain, lack of concentration, panic attacks, memory loss and depression that usually follows a viral infection.

Mucous membrane Any of the membranes rich in mucous glands that line body passages such as the nose.

Opiate Any substance that induces rest or quiets uneasiness.

Osteoporosis A disease involving the weakening of bone that is caused by a loss of calcium.

Papain An enzyme present in the juice of papayas that breaks down proteins.

Parkinson's Disease Progressive nervous disease marked by tremor, weakness of resting muscles and a peculiar gait.

Pectin Soluble fibre that adds bulk and soothes the gut. Apples are particularly rich in pectin.

Phytochemical Any of the natural chemicals that occur in plants.

Phytoestrogen Any of the oestrogen-like chemicals that naturally occur in plants.

Pinene A beneficial substance similar to limonene (see above) that is found mainly in tropical fruits.

Probiotic bacteria Beneficial bacteria.

Seasonal Affective Disorder (SAD) Disorder in which a person's moods change with the seasons, most pointedly showing depression in winter.

Salicylate Bitter-tasting substance found in plants (eg willow bark) that is used to reduce fever.

Sinigrin An antibiotic volatile oil found in horseradish that is particularly protective and stimulating to the mucous membranes.

Tannin Any of the soluble, astringent substances found in plants.

Terpene A substance found in essential oils, such as those present in conifers.

Thujone A volatile oil that is beneficial in small doses.

Toxin A poisonous substance produced by bacteria.

Uric acid A crystalline acid that occurs in the urine of most animals. Too much uric acid in the bloodstream can collect in the joints, causing intense pain.

Virus Any agent that causes an infectious disease.

Xeaxanthine A carotenoid that is of particular benefit to the eyes.

Zingiberene Beneficial volatile oil found in ginger that stimulates circulation.

index

Entries in **bold** are juice names.

author's note

My thanks are due to Mitchell Beazley, and particularly to my commissioning editor, Margaret Little, who waged a titanic struggle against great odds and the demands of my many commitments. Thankfully, her combined use of sticks and carrots – essential for a juicing book! – got the manuscript finished. Editor Jamie Ambrose worked tirelessly, uncomplainingly and always with a sense of humour through the entire text. And, as always, my desperately overworked secretary Janet burnt lots of midnight oil and drank far too many cups of midnight coffee to help me write this book.
Without all of them, it would never have seen the light of day.

michael van straten